THE COMPLEAT CHICKEN COOKBOOK

THE COMPLEAT CHICKEN COOKBOOK

ANNE M. FLETCHER

AN ESSANDESS SPECIAL EDITION
NEW YORK

THE COMPLEAT CHICKEN COOKBOOK
SBN: 671-10459-4
Copyright, ©, 1970 by Anne M. Fletcher.

All rights reserved.
Published by ESSANDESS SPECIAL EDITONS,
a division of Simon & Schuster, Inc.,
630 Fifth Avenue, New York, N.Y. 10020,
and on the same day in Canada by Simon & Schuster
of Canada, Ltd., Richmond Hill, Ontario.

PRINTED IN THE U.S.A.

CONTENTS

1. *Chicken—The World's Favorite Bird* 1
2. *Appetizers* 11
3. *Soups* 15
4. *Baked and Fried Chicken* 23
5. *Broiled and Grilled Chicken* 31
6. *Roasts with Stuffings* 39
7. *Stews* 49
8. *Casseroles* 57
9. *Skillet Entrees* 69
10. *Chicken Breasts* 79
11. *Creamed Chicken* 89
12. *Around the World* 97
13. *Winebibber's Corner* 121
14. *Game Hens* 129
15. *Salads* 137
16. *Sandwiches* 145

Index 151

1
CHICKEN— THE WORLD'S FAVORITE BIRD

The Story of the Chicken

Everybody the world over loves chicken. With the possible exception of the Arctic Circle or the Sahara Desert, you're bound to find a chicken in the pot in every land. There's hardly a region that doesn't produce this ubiquitous creature, or a religion that forbids its consumption. Whether served delicately laced with Sauterne or pungently spiced in the Creole manner, it retains its distinctive appeal. Who doesn't recall the aroma of a steaming cup of Mama's strength-restoring chicken broth, or the finger-licking goodness of a golden-brown barbecued drumstick? Chicken can be cooked in hundreds of ways; no matter what your preference is, there's a chicken recipe to satisfy it.

Man has been cooking chicken for over 4,000 years. It is believed that the most important ancestor of today's chicken was a small red bird that lived in the jungles of southeast Asia and was first tamed and raised for food nearly 5,000 years ago; the chicken was probably fully domesticated by 2000 B.C. As man traveled to new areas, chickens went along. They are mentioned in Chinese scrolls dating back to 1400 B.C. and appeared in Egypt about the same time; they were mentioned frequently in Greek and Roman literature. Today the chicken is the most numerous bird in the world, with more than 200 varieties in existence. Some are bred to produce better eggs, and others for tastier meat.

Spanish explorers carried live chickens on their ships and brought them to the New World in the 1500s. Since 1607, when settlers in Jamestown, Virginia, started raising chickens, chicken farming has spread across the United States, until now the country raises over 2½ billion meat chickens, more than one-fifth of the world's supply and more than any other single country.

Although families in farm areas have always raised chickens for eggs, meat, and profit, it is only since the early 1900s that farms in the United States have specialized in raising chickens. Crossbreeding, scientific feeding, improved control of disease, and more efficient marketing techniques have vastly improved the quality of the chickens available to the American consumer, who now eats about 35 pounds of chicken meat a year.

Why Buy Chicken?

Versatility is surely the chicken's greatest attribute. A small change in seasoning can result in a completely new taste, allowing a limitless number of possibilities for the imaginative cook. However, there are other important reasons for its popularity. First, compared with other meats, chicken has excellent nutritive values. It not only is high in protein, vitamin A, niacin, and calcium, but it also is lower in calories and saturated fats than most other meats. It is healthful, easily digestible, and appealing to even the most delicate appetite.

Of equal importance to the consumer is the cost factor. At the present time the average cost of broilers on the market is under 40¢ per pound. There are bones, of course, but even when these are removed, the cost per edible pound (fat and bones removed) is still at least a dollar less than the cost per edible pound of such meats as pork chops or bottom round steak. Surely chicken is an excellent bargain!

CHICKEN—THE WORLD'S FAVORITE BIRD

How To Insure Freshness

For the most flavor, fresh chicken should come from the farm to your table in the least amount of time. The key factor is the distance between the grower or processor and the meat market. If the label on a packaged fresh chicken indicates a local grower, you may be sure that the chicken has been "on the road" for a shorter period of time than one that has been shipped long distances, and that it will be fresher. Generally, chicken is sold fresh, but some processors quick-freeze chicken as soon as it has been dressed. This type of chicken will be as fresh as a locally grown one.

If you wish to stock a supply of chickens when prices are irresistibly low, you can easily freeze your own, which then may be stored up to 6 months. First, place the chicken in an airtight plastic bag, squeeze out the excess air, and seal the bag. Wrap the bag in freezer paper, seal it with tape, and place it in the quick-freeze section of your home freezer for 12 to 24 hours; then transfer it to the freezer storage bin. To cook the chicken, unwrap it and let it thaw (4 to 6 hours for a normal broiler-fryer), and then cook it immediately. It will keep all of its farm-fresh quality.

What Type of Chicken Should You Buy?

The most popular purchase is the *broiler-fryer*, a chicken of either sex that is usually from 6 to 13 weeks old. These lean, tender birds can attain a weight of 4 pounds in this short period of time through scientific feeding, although they may be marketed as small as 1½ pounds. They are available whole, split, cut up, or in parts.

Chickens kept on the farm until the age of 4 to 6 months are called *roasters*; they usually weigh 3 to 5 pounds. They are sold whole so that they may be stuffed, trussed, and roasted. Hens that have completed their egg-laying cycle are used as *stewing chickens*. They are available whole or cut up, and are often used in soups and stews. They may weigh 3 to 6 pounds.

CHICKEN—THE WORLD'S FAVORITE BIRD

Capons are castrated male chickens that have been especially fed to grow large and meaty; they often weigh as much as 7 or 8 pounds and are excellent roasted. The *Rock Cornish game hen*, on the other hand, is a miniature chicken, with an average weight of 1 pound; it is usually marketed at 6 weeks. It has a very delicate flavor, and is generally stuffed, roasted, and served one to a person.

How Much Will You Need?

There may be slight variations, depending on how the chicken is cooked, but generally servings are calculated as follows:

3- to 3½-pound chicken	4 servings
1- to 2-pound chicken	2 servings
Rock Cornish game hen	1 serving
Whole chicken breast*	1 serving
Thigh and drumstick	1 serving
3-pound cooked chicken	2½ cups diced meat

How To Prepare a Chicken for Cooking

Cleaning. Fortunately, most chicken buyers no longer have to face the job of plucking feathers, pulling gizzards, and singeing hair. Meat markets now sell poultry fully dressed, with the giblets separately wrapped in the package. However, chickens still should be cleaned just before cooking. Whole chickens should be rinsed inside and out with lukewarm water, to which a tablespoon of baking soda may be added. But be careful never to soak a chicken in water! Instead, drain it and pat it dry with paper towels. This method may also be used for chicken parts, or you may

---

* This constitutes all the breast meat of one chicken. A split breast is half of a whole chicken breast.

CHICKEN—THE WORLD'S FAVORITE BIRD

omit the washing, and instead rub all sides of the chicken with a cut lemon to clean it.

Cutting. You may find it more economical to buy whole chickens and cut them up yourself. To do this, you will only need a sharp knife and poultry shears. Fryers are cut up as follows:

1. Bend one wing forward until the joint shows. Cut toward the joint, break it, and finish cutting the wing off. Repeat on the other side.
2. Pull one leg and thigh away from the body and cut through the skin to the thigh joint. Break the joint and finish cutting the leg off. Repeat on the other side.
3. Separate the thighs from the drumsticks by cutting toward the joint. Break the joint and finish cutting.
4. Using shears, clip below all rib joints on both sides of the body toward the shoulder joints. Break the joints and finish cutting.
5. To split the whole breast, snip lengthwise through the ribs just beside the breastbone.
6. Cut the back just behind the last rib; using your hands, break the joint, then finish cutting.

Cutting Broiler Halves

1. Laying the chicken breast side up, start at the neck and cut or snip the full length of the breast, just beside the breastbone.
2. Spread the chicken apart, skin side down.
3. Cut the ribs just beside the backbone and cut through the pelvis on the opposite side from the breast cut, so that each half will have a bone ridge.

Boning. Some recipes call for either the whole chicken or the breast to be boned. In many instances the butcher will perform this service, but if you prefer to do it yourself, here is the procedure:

1. Cut the wings off at the elbow.
2. Starting at the neck, make an incision along the backbone and along each side of the tail to the opening.

CHICKEN—THE WORLD'S FAVORITE BIRD

3. Using a sharp, pointed knife and pushing with your fingers, cut the skin-covered flesh away from the back and ribs to the ridge of the backbone.
4. Insert the tip of the knife into each hip joint and turn it until the joint breaks. Break the wing joints at the shoulder in the same way.
5. Loosen the meat and skin from the muscle above the hip joint, leaving the legs and wings attached.
6. Pull the remaining meat away from the breastbone, leaving the legs and wings attached, until the two halves are connected only at the rear opening and below the tip of the breastbone. Separate the halves by cutting through the thin layer of flesh and skin.
7. To remove the bones from the thighs, legs, and wings, work down from the inside of the body, leaving the outside skin uncut. Cut through the flesh to the bone, loosening the flesh by scraping along the bone. Cut through the knee joints and pull out the thigh bones.
8. Cut away a circle of skin above the joint at the thin end of each drumstick. Hold the drumstick at right angles to the table and scrape the flesh loose from the bone. Pull the bones out.
9. Remove the wing bones in the same manner.
10. Carve away the wishbone, which has remained in the breast.

Stuffing. If a boned chicken is to be stuffed, place the meat skin side down, sprinkle it with salt, and place the stuffing in the center. Overlap each half over the center and fold down the neck skin. Tie three strings around the body across the breast. Brush the chicken with melted shortening and roast according to recipe directions.

To stuff a roasting chicken, first prepare your favorite stuffing recipe, allowing 1¼ cups of dressing per pound of chicken. Rinse the chicken well inside and out. Insert your fingers into the cavity and remove any remaining bits of viscera, then rinse again. Drain the inside well and dry the outside with paper towels. Sprinkle the cavity lightly with salt. Place the stuffing in the neck cavity to fill

CHICKEN — THE WORLD'S FAVORITE BIRD

out breast area; pull up the neck skin and fasten it to the back of the chicken with skewers. The job will be made easier if you place the chicken in a bowl to keep it from slipping.

Stuff the body cavity loosely, about four-fifths full, since the dressing will expand during cooking. Place skewers across the body opening and lace it shut with string. Now the chicken is ready for trussing.

Trussing. To truss a roasting chicken, tie the wing tips together over the back of the chicken with a piece of string, then tie the drumsticks together and fasten the string around the tail.

Carving. To carve a roasted chicken, follow these steps:

1. Untie the drumsticks and remove the skewers and string from the cavities.
2. Remove one drumstick and thigh by firmly holding them together and pulling them away from the body. Cut through the skin between the leg and body. With the flat side of a knife, press the leg down until the joint is visible. Cut through the joint, then through the meat to the back. Repeat with the other leg.
3. Place the legs on a warm serving platter and cut through the knee joints to separate the drumsticks from the thighs.
4. Cut into the white meat in front of and parallel to one wing. Cut deeply into the joint, then slice away to separate the wing from the body. Repeat with the other wing and place them on the platter.
5. Starting from the front at the fattest part of the body, cut thin slices of white meat parallel to the wing cut. Continue to slice until there are enough servings or until no more meat remains.
6. Repeat this procedure on the second side. Remove the wishbone by inserting the knife under it and giving it a twist. Trim the wishbone away from the breast, then carve off the white meat.
7. Turn the carcass upside down and trim any remaining meat from this side.
8. Remove the stuffing with a spoon and pile it loosely into a heated serving bowl.

CHICKEN—THE WORLD'S FAVORITE BIRD

Roasting Time and Temperature Chart

The newest method of roasting a chicken employs a steady, low oven temperature. This method produces juicier, more tender results than the old method, which called for browning the chicken at a high temperature, then reducing the heat and baking.

Weigh the chicken after it has been stuffed. Multiply the weight by the minutes per pound given in the table below, using the lower figure for large birds and the higher figure for small birds. This time chart is based on the meat being at room temperature. If it has been refrigerated, add 15 to 30 minutes to the total cooking time.

TYPE OF CHICKEN	OVEN TEMPERATURE	MINUTES PER POUND
Rock Cornish game hen	350 degrees	20 to 22
Roasting chicken	300 degrees	30 to 35
Capon	325 degrees	22 to 30

General Rules for Cooking Chicken

Frying

1. Rinse the cut-up chicken parts; drain and dry with paper towels.
2. Shake two or three pieces at a time in a paper or plastic bag with the coating mixture called for by the recipe.
3. Heat ¼ inch of oil in a large frying pan until a drop of water sizzles, or in an electric skillet at the recommended frying temperature.
4. Brown the large pieces on both sides, turning with kitchen tongs; fit the smaller pieces in between. This step should take 15 to 20 minutes.
5. Reduce the heat to a simmer and cover the pan tightly. Cook for another 15 to 20 minutes, or until the largest pieces are fork-tender. Turn the chicken once during this time.
6. Remove the cover and cook for 5 to 10 minutes longer to re-crisp the skin.

CHICKEN—THE WORLD'S FAVORITE BIRD

Broiling and Grilling. Since both methods cook the chicken by direct, dry heat, it is essential for the meat to be kept moist by frequent basting, either with melted shortening or a prepared sauce. To insure even browning, the chicken should lie flat. This can be accomplished by breaking the wing, hip, and knee joints and tucking in the wing tips on the cut side. The chicken halves or quarters should be washed and patted dry before cooking.

Oven Method of Broiling

1. Preheat the broiler. Lay the chicken, skin side down, in a broiler pan (not on a rack). Baste the chicken generously and season it lightly with salt and pepper. Place it about 6 inches from the heat. This distance may be increased if the chicken is browning too quickly.
2. Broil the chicken 20 to 25 minutes, basting often, until it is nicely browned.
3. Turn it skin side up, baste it, season it, and broil 15 to 20 minutes more, basting frequently. The chicken is done when the drumsticks twist easily.

Cooking a Chicken on a Charcoal Grill

1. Set the greased grill 6 to 8 inches above the coals, so that the cooking temperature is about 325 degrees.
2. Baste the chicken generously on both sides and place it skin side up on the grill. Baste often and turn it several times with tongs. Cook 45 to 60 minutes, depending on the size, until the chicken is tender and the joints twist easily.

Roasting. The average roasting chicken weighs 3 to 5 pounds. If the chicken is to be stuffed, weigh it with the dressing and allow a roasting time of 30 to 35 minutes per pound; a smaller chicken might require only 25 to 30 minutes per pound. Have the chicken at room temperature before stuffing and roasting it. Never stuff poultry very long before you are ready to roast it. Wash the chicken and dry it with paper towels, then fill it with your favorite stuffing, following the instructions given above. The openings can easily be closed with metal skewers, or they can be sewn shut. Truss the chicken by folding back the wings and tying with string, then tying together the tips of the drumsticks. Place the chicken breast side up in a roasting pan, preferably one with a drip-rack; sprinkle with salt and brush with melted butter. Be careful **not to** pierce the skin with a fork or you will lose valuable juices. Bake at 300 degrees, basting every 10 minutes, until the legs move easily and the chicken is nicely browned. A flavorful basting sauce may be made by combining ¼ cup melted butter with ¼ cup dry sherry; the sauce should be kept warm during roasting time. Remove the chicken to a warm carving platter and use the drippings for gravy.

Stewing

1. Place the whole or cut-up chicken in a Dutch oven with a tight-fitting lid. Add seasonings according to the recipe and water to cover.
2. Bring the water to a boil, skim off the foam, reduce the heat to a simmer, and cover.
3. Cook until the meatiest parts are fork-tender, about 45 to 50 minutes. Remove the pot from the heat, place the chicken on a plate to cool, and strain the broth.

2
APPETIZERS

CHICKEN LIVER HORS D'OEUVRES

1 cup flour
⅛ teaspoon salt
6 ounces (1½ sticks) butter
3 tablespoons sour cream
4 chicken livers
½ cup diced mushrooms
½ teaspoon garlic salt
⅛ teaspoon pepper

Sift flour and salt together into a bowl and cut in 1 stick of butter until well blended. Add sour cream and mix until smooth. Wrap dough in waxed paper and chill overnight. The next day, melt remaining butter in a small saucepan; add chicken livers, mushrooms, and seasonings and simmer for 10 minutes. Cool 15 minutes, then chop livers fine.

Roll chilled dough on a lightly floured board until it is ⅛ inch thick; cut rounds with a cookie cutter. Place 1 heaping teaspoon of the liver mixture on each round, fold over, and seal tightly. Set pastries on a baking sheet and place in a 375-degree oven for 20 minutes. Serve hot. *Serves 6.*

APPETIZERS

CHICKEN LIVERS *EN BROCHETTE*

2½ pounds chicken livers
2 tablespoons butter
2 medium onions, sliced
1½ teaspoons salt
¼ teaspoon pepper

1 tablespoon minced parsley
Small bay leaf
¼ teaspoon thyme
6 slices bacon

Quickly brown chicken livers in butter, tossing well. Add 1 cup water and all other ingredients except bacon; cover and simmer for 15 minutes or until tender. Remove the chicken livers. Thread one end of a slice of bacon on each of 6 skewers. Divide chicken livers among skewers, then wind bacon around livers and secure on the other end of the skewers. Place on charcoal grill, turning often, until bacon is crisp. *Serves 6.*

CHICKEN TIMBALES WITH TOMATO SAUCE

2 cups uncooked ground white chicken meat
1 tablespoon finely chopped parsley
1 teaspoon salt

¼ teaspoon celery salt
Dash pepper or paprika
3 eggs, separated
⅔ cup heavy cream

Combine chicken with parsley, salt, celery salt, and pepper. Beat egg yolks lightly and blend into mixture, then slowly stir in cream. Whip egg whites until stiff and fold into mixture. Butter 6 custard cups and fill each two-thirds full. Place in a pan of hot water to the level of the custard mixture and bake in a 350-degree oven for 40 minutes. Meanwhile, prepare tomato sauce.

TOMATO SAUCE:

2 tablespoons butter
2 tablespoons minced onion
2 tablespoons minced celery

1 can condensed tomato soup, undiluted
2 tablespoons chicken broth or hot water

Sauté onion and celery in butter until tender, then stir in tomato soup and chicken broth. Heat slowly, but do not allow to boil. When timbales are done, invert and serve with sauce. *Serves 6.*

CRISP ORIENTAL APPETIZERS

1 pound chicken livers, quartered	1 cup flour
	½ teaspoon baking powder
¼ cup soy sauce	1 teaspoon salt
¼ cup dry sherry	Oil for frying

Marinate chicken livers in the combined soy sauce and sherry for at least 30 minutes. Make a batter from the flour, ⅔ cup water, baking powder, and salt; drain livers and dip into batter to coat. Preheat deep oil to 375 degrees and fry livers for 3 minutes, or until lightly browned. Drain, spear with toothpicks, and serve hot. *Serves 6.*

PICNIC PÂTÉ

6 ounces (1½ sticks) butter, softened	1 teaspoon salt
	⅔ cup Riesling
1 pound chicken livers	1 teaspoon garlic puree
½ pound fresh mushrooms	½ teaspoon dry mustard
⅓ cup finely sliced green onion, white part only	Pinch crumbled rosemary
	Pinch dill weed

Melt ½ stick butter in a skillet. Add chicken livers, mushrooms, onion, and salt and simmer for 10 minutes, stirring occasionally. Add Riesling, garlic puree, mustard, rosemary, and dill weed. Cover and cook slowly for 10 minutes more, or until chicken livers and mushrooms are very tender and almost all the liquid has been absorbed. Cool slightly; whirl in a blender until smooth. Blend in remaining stick of softened butter and add more salt if needed. Pack into a crock and chill at least 8 hours. *Makes 1½ pints.*

APPETIZERS

PÂTÉ DE FOIE

1 pound chicken livers
1 medium onion, peeled and quartered
¾ cup melted butter
4 tablespoons grated onion
2 teaspoons salt
½ teaspoon pepper
¼ teaspoon mace
1 tablespoon dry mustard
¼ teaspoon anchovy paste
1 tablespoon brandy

Wash and trim chicken livers. Place livers in a saucepan with onion quarters and 2 cups water; cover and simmer for 20 minutes. Drain, remove onion, and discard it. Grind livers in a food chopper at least 3 times, until very fine. Add remaining ingredients and mix into a smooth paste. Press firmly into a mold and chill for no less than 3 hours. Unmold onto a plate just before serving. Excellent with sliced sour French bread. *Serves 6.*

3
SOUPS

CONTINENTAL CHICKEN SOUP

1 4-pound stewing chicken
1 lemon, quartered
1 medium onion, peeled
4 cloves
Fresh minced parsley
2 teaspoons salt
¼ teaspoon pepper
¼ teaspoon crushed thyme
1 bay leaf
½ cup minced leeks or green onion
½ cup diced celery
½ cup diced carrot
2 cups Sauterne

Wash and dry chicken. Rub inside and out with lemon wedges, squeezing to release juice. Place chicken in a large saucepan and cover with 1 quart water. Stud whole onion with cloves; add to saucepan with 1 tablespoon minced parsley and remaining ingredients. Bring to a boil, reduce heat, cover, and simmer for 1 to 1½ hours, or until chicken is tender. Remove chicken from broth and strip away skin and bones. Cut meat into bite-sized pieces and place in a large soup tureen. Strain broth over chicken and serve sprinkled with fresh minced parsley. *Serves 6.*

SOUPS

CHICKEN WON TON SOUP

2 cups sifted flour
1½ teaspoons salt
2 eggs
1½ cups cooked, finely chopped chicken, plus 1 cup cooked slivered chicken
2 teaspoons soy sauce
¼ teaspoon pepper
2 green onions, finely chopped
8 cups rich chicken broth
½ pound raw spinach, shredded

Sift flour and salt together twice. Beat eggs well and stir in ⅓ cup water. Slowly add eggs to flour and blend well. Knead dough on a floured board until smooth and set aside. For the filling, combine chopped chicken, soy sauce, pepper, and green onions, mixing well. Roll dough on floured board as thin as possible, then cut into 4-inch squares. Place a heaping teaspoonful of filling on each square, wet edges with a bit of water, and seal diagonally. Set each triangle on its long edge and turn up ends to make a butterfly shape. Place triangles in 2 quarts boiling salted water and cook for 10 to 15 minutes. When won ton rise to the top, they are done. Drain and keep warm. Heat chicken broth and add slivered chicken and spinach. Cook for 2 minutes. Divide won ton among 6 soup bowls, pour chicken soup over them, and serve. *Serves 6.*

CHICKEN MUSHROOM SOUP

6 cups chicken broth
½ cup chopped celery
½ cup chopped onion
½ pound fresh mushrooms, sliced
1 cup chopped cooked white chicken meat
½ teaspoon salt
2 tablespoons soy sauce
2 eggs, well beaten

Heat chicken broth. Meanwhile, whirl celery and onion in a blender until smooth. Add to broth and simmer for 5 minutes. Add mushrooms and chicken and simmer 10 minutes longer, then add salt and soy sauce. Slowly drizzle in eggs, cook 1 minute, and serve immediately. *Serves 6.*

CHICKEN BROTH

1 4- to 5-pound chicken
1 medium onion, quartered
4 stalks celery with leaves
1 whole carrot
6 sprigs parsley
1 tablespoon salt
½ teaspoon pepper
½ teaspoon poultry seasoning
1 bay leaf

Place all ingredients in a large saucepan or Dutch oven with 12 cups water, and bring to a boil. Reduce heat, cover, and cook for 1 hour or longer, until chicken is tender. Remove chicken from broth and allow to cool enough to handle; remove meat for other purposes, but return skin and bones to broth. Continue to simmer 1½ hours more. Allow to cool, strain broth, and refrigerate until fat forms a solid layer on top, then skim off fat. *Makes about 6 cups of broth.*

CREOLE CHICKEN GUMBO

1 3-pound fryer, cut up
½ pound smoked ham, cubed
1 medium onion, peeled
1 bay leaf
1 sprig thyme
6 large tomatoes
4 cups sliced okra
½ red pepper, seeded and chopped
½ cup chopped parsley
4 tablespoons butter
2 teaspoons salt
1½ teaspoons filé (optional)

Place chicken in a large saucepan with ham, onion, bay leaf, thyme, and 3 pints water. Cook, covered, for 1 hour. Meanwhile peel tomatoes and chop very fine; drain off juice and reserve. Sauté tomato pulp, okra, chopped red pepper, and parsley in butter over a low flame for 10 minutes, stirring now and then to prevent sticking. Season with salt and filé, add tomato juice, and simmer, covered, 10 minutes longer. When chicken is done, remove from broth, let it cool until it can be handled, then remove skin and bones. Cut chicken into cubes and return to broth. Add vegetable mixture to chicken and simmer, covered, for 15 minutes. Remove bay leaf and thyme before serving. *Serves 8.*

SOUPS

HURRY-UP MULLIGATAWNY

1 can condensed chicken with rice soup, undiluted
1 can pepper pot soup
1 soup can milk
¼ teaspoon curry powder
Sprigs of parsley

Combine soups and milk in a saucepan and stir in curry powder. Simmer slowly (do not boil) until heated through. Serve topped with parsley. *Serves 4.*

CHILLED CHICKEN-CUCUMBER SOUP

3 cups rich chicken broth
1 tablespoon melted chicken fat or butter
2 cups coarsely chopped cucumber
4 green onions, chopped
½ teaspoon seasoned salt
2 tablespoons lemon juice
¼ cup dry sherry
Sour cream

Place all ingredients except sour cream in blender; whirl until smooth. Pour into a saucepan and bring to a boil. Remove from heat, let cool, then chill for several hours in the refrigerator. Stir before serving and top each bowl or cup with a spoonful of sour cream. *Serves 4.*

CREAM OF CHICKEN SOUP

3 tablespoons butter
3 tablespoons flour
3 cups hot chicken broth
2 cups hot milk
1 egg yolk, slightly beaten
1 teaspoon salt
Dash paprika
1 tablespoon minced parsley
½ cup minced cooked chicken (optional)

Melt butter in a saucepan; stir in flour, slowly blend in chicken broth and milk, and stir until slightly thickened and smooth; do not allow to boil. Pour a little of the soup over the egg yolk, stir, and return to soup. Add seasonings and, if desired, chicken. Heat over low flame for 2 to 3 minutes. *Serves 4 to 6.*

SOUPS

BELGIAN CHICKEN SOUP

2 2-pound broilers, split with giblets
2 pounds veal bones
1 celery root
6 sprigs parsley
2 celery stalks
2 tablespoons salt
½ teaspoon pepper
1 lemon, peeled and thinly sliced
2 cups white wine
4 tablespoons butter
2 tablespoons chopped chives

In a saucepan combine chicken giblets, veal bones, 6 cups water, celery root, parsley, celery stalks, salt, pepper, and lemon slices. When boiling, skim top, cover, and cook slowly for 2 hours. Strain, reserving liquid. Wash chicken halves and place in saucepan. Cover with reserved stock and white wine, add butter, and simmer for 45 minutes or until chicken is done. Remove chicken and cut into serving pieces. Place a piece in each soup plate, cover with soup, and sprinkle with chives. *Serves 6.*

WINTER HARVEST SOUP

1 2- to 2½-pound chicken, cut up
2 pounds beef stew meat
2 tablespoons plus 2 teaspoons salt
1 clove garlic
1 medium onion, peeled and quartered
4 medium potatoes, pared and diced
4 medium sweet potatoes, pared and diced
4 carrots, diced
1 cup diced zucchini or other squash
1 cup drained kernel corn
1 cup shredded cabbage
1 cup cut green beans or peas
¼ cup sliced leeks
Freshly ground pepper to taste
¼ teaspoon oregano
6 tablespoons uncooked long-grain white rice

Place chicken, stew meat, 3 quarts water, 2 tablespoons salt, garlic, and onion in a very large saucepan. Bring to a boil, skim top,

SOUPS

reduce heat, and cover. Simmer for 1 hour, then remove meat to cool. Strain broth and pour back into saucepan. Remove skin and bones from chicken and fat from beef and cut into bite-sized pieces. Return meat to broth and heat. When boiling, add rest of vegetables, 2 teaspoons salt, pepper, and oregano, and bring back to a boil. Reduce heat, cover, and cook for 20 minutes. Add rice and cook 20 minutes longer. *Serves 10 to 12.*

ORIENTAL CHICKEN-CORN SOUP

2 quarts chicken broth
2 cups minced cooked chicken
2 tablespoons dry sherry
2 egg whites, lightly beaten
1 1-pound can cream-style corn
½ teaspoon monosodium glutamate
1 teaspoon salt
¼ teaspoon pepper

Bring chicken broth to a boil. Meanwhile combine chicken, sherry, and egg whites, and add to broth. After a minute, skim top and reduce heat; add corn and seasonings and simmer for 5 minutes. *Serves 8.*

SCOTCH CHICKEN-LEEK SOUP

1 5-pound stewing hen, cut up
2 tablespoons salt
½ teaspoon pepper
½ teaspoon poultry seasoning
1 bay leaf
1 dozen leeks or 18 fresh green onions
1½ cups half-cooked long-grain white rice

Wash chicken and place in a large saucepan with 2½ quarts water and seasonings; cook for 2 hours. Remove chicken pieces, slice leeks, and add with rice to the soup. Cook for 25 minutes. Meanwhile, remove chicken from bones and break meat into small pieces. Return meat to soup and cook 10 minutes longer. This soup is very thick and can be served as a main dish. *Serves 6.*

MATZO-BALL SOUP

1 stewing chicken
1 medium onion, peeled and quartered
3 stalks celery with leaves
2 carrots
6 sprigs parsley
1 tablespoon salt

Place all ingredients in a large saucepan with 2 quarts water and bring to a boil. Skim top, reduce heat, and cook, covered, for 1½ hours, or until chicken is tender. Remove chicken and use for other purposes. Strain broth through a fine-meshed sieve or cheesecloth, and chill until fat solidifies on top. Remove fat and save for later use. Meanwhile prepare matzo balls.

MATZO BALLS:

2 eggs
¾ teaspoon salt
⅛ teaspoon white pepper
¼ cup melted chicken fat
¼ cup chicken broth
1 tablespoon minced parsley
¾ cup matzo meal

Beat eggs in a small bowl with a rotary beater. Add salt, pepper, chicken fat, and broth, and beat thoroughly. Stir in parsley and matzo meal until blended; batter will be stiff. Chill for at least 1 hour. Roll tiny balls, using a level teaspoon of batter for each. If they seem very soft, chill for 30 minutes before cooking. When they are ready, heat broth to boiling and adjust seasoning with salt and pepper if necessary. Drop balls into boiling broth, reduce heat, cover, and simmer for 25 minutes. *Serves 6.*

4

BAKED AND FRIED CHICKEN

Baked Chicken

CHICKEN MARYLAND

2 broiler-fryers, cut up, with giblets
1 teaspoon dehydrated vegetable flakes
1 teaspoon celery salt
½ cup flour
1 teaspoon salt
½ teaspoon paprika
2 eggs, lightly beaten
¼ cup milk
½ cup fine dry bread crumbs
½ cup salad oil

Place giblets and backs from chickens in 1½ cups water with seasoning to make chicken broth. Simmer for 1 hour. Strain, reserving 1 cup broth. Combine flour with salt and paprika in a bag; shake chicken pieces in the bag, a few at a time, until all are dusted. Combine eggs and milk in a shallow dish and dip chicken in the mixture, then roll in bread crumbs. Allow crumbs to dry for 1 hour. Heat oil in a large, heavy skillet and brown as many pieces

BAKED AND FRIED CHICKEN

as possible without crowding. Drain chicken pieces, reserving ¼ cup of drippings and set pieces in a large, shallow baking dish. Continue until all pieces are browned, then bake uncovered at 350 degrees for 45 minutes. Meanwhile, prepare cream gravy.

CREAM GRAVY:

¼ cup reserved drippings
¼ cup flour
1 cup reserved chicken broth
2 cups half and half
2 egg yolks

In the ¼ cup of reserved drippings in the skillet, stir in flour, blend in reserved chicken broth and half and half, and stir until thickened; strain into a small saucepan. Lightly beat egg yolks, add a little of the cream gravy, then return to pan. When chicken is ready, heat gravy over low flame but do not boil, and season with salt and pepper to taste. *Serves 6.*

CURRY-GLAZED CHICKEN

CURRY GLAZE:

6 slices bacon
½ cup chopped onion
2 tablespoons flour
1 can condensed beef broth, undiluted
3 tablespoons lemon juice
1 tablespoon sugar
1 tablespoon curry powder
2 tablespoons catsup
3 tablespoons applesauce
3 tablespoons flaked coconut

Fry bacon until crisp; drain and mince. Remove all but 2 tablespoons bacon drippings from pan, then sauté onions until limp. Return bacon bits to pan, stir in flour, and add beef broth and lemon juice, blending well. Add remaining ingredients in order, stirring continuously until thickened. Set aside.

CHICKEN:

½ cup flour
1½ teaspoons salt
1½ teaspoons ground ginger
2 broilers, split and quartered
6 tablespoons melted butter

Combine flour, salt, and ginger in a paper bag. Shake chicken pieces until coated, then dip in melted butter to cover. Arrange skin side up in a large baking dish and place uncovered in a 400-degree oven for 20 minutes, or until chicken is light gold. Brush on half of curry glaze, reduce heat to 325 degrees, and bake 20 minutes more. Brush with remaining glaze and bake for another 20 minutes. *Serves 8.*

DEVILED CHICKEN WINGS

1½ pounds chicken wings
½ cup melted butter
1 teaspoon prepared mustard
1 teaspoon wine vinegar
1 cup fine bread crumbs
½ teaspoon salt
½ teaspoon paprika

Wash and dry chicken wings. Combine melted butter with mustard and vinegar; combine bread crumbs with salt and paprika. Dip wings into butter mixture, then roll in seasoned bread crumbs. Place on a baking sheet and bake uncovered at 350 degrees for 40 minutes, or until crisp and fork-tender. *Serves 4.*

EASY TARRAGON CHICKEN

1 large frying chicken, cut up
1 large onion, chopped
1½ teaspoons tarragon
¼ teaspoon poultry seasoning
2 teaspoons salt
¼ teaspoon pepper
1 can condensed cream of chicken soup, undiluted
½ cup milk
½ cup slivered blanched almonds

Wash and dry chicken pieces, then place them, skin side up and not touching, in a large, shallow baking dish. Combine all remaining ingredients except almonds and pour over chicken. Bake uncovered at 375 degrees for 40 minutes. Sprinkle slivered almonds on top and continue baking for 10 minutes, or until chicken is tender. *Serves 4.*

BAKED AND FRIED CHICKEN

GARLIC-BAKED CHICKEN

2 small broilers, split
4 ounces (1 stick) butter, softened
1 tablespoon packaged dry garlic salad dressing mix
1 cup fine dry cracker crumbs

Wash chicken halves and pat dry. Cream butter with salad dressing mix and spread over chicken. Dip chicken into cracker crumbs and place, skin side up and not touching, on a large shallow baking sheet. Bake uncovered at 400 degrees for 1¼ hours, or until fork-tender. *Serves 4.*

OLD-FASHIONED OVEN-FRIED CHICKEN

3 fryers, cut up
1½ cups light cream
1 cup flour
1½ cups packaged cornflake crumbs
2 teaspoons seasoned salt
2 teaspoons paprika
¼ teaspoon pepper
1 cup salad oil

Wash and dry chicken pieces and dip in cream. Combine flour, cornflake crumbs, seasoned salt, paprika, and pepper in a paper sack; shake a few pieces of chicken at a time in this mixture until well coated. Heat oil in a deep skillet and brown chicken on both sides. Place chicken in a large roasting pan, cover, and bake at 350 degrees for 45 minutes. Remove cover and continue baking 15 minutes more. *Serves 10.*

TASTY TARRAGON WINGS

16 chicken wings
1 tablespoon monosodium glutamate
2 teaspoons salt
1½ teaspoons dry crumbled tarragon
3 tablespoons butter

Place chicken wings in one layer in a shallow baking pan. Sprinkle with monosodium glutamate, salt, and tarragon, and dot with butter. Bake uncovered at 375 degrees for 45 minutes, basting occasionally with drippings. *Serves 4.*

OVEN-BARBECUED CHICKEN

2 fryers, cut up
1 medium onion, chopped
2 tablespoons butter
¼ cup lemon juice
1 cup bottled chili sauce
½ cup chopped green olives
2 tablespoons light brown sugar
1 teaspoon salt
¼ teaspoon paprika

Wash chicken pieces and pat dry. Place in one layer in a large baking dish, skin side up, and bake, uncovered, in a 350-degree oven, for 30 minutes. Meanwhile, sauté onion in butter until tender. Add ½ cup water and remaining ingredients; blend well, cover, and simmer for 20 minutes. Pour sauce over chicken, cover, and bake for 15 minutes, then uncover, baste with sauce, and bake for 15 more minutes, basting occasionally. *Serves 6.*

SIMPLY DELICIOUS BAKED CHICKEN

2 broiling chickens, split
4 ounces (1 stick) butter
½ cup dry white wine
1 teaspoon salt
¼ teaspoon pepper
½ teaspoon dried tarragon
2 teaspoons cornstarch

Place chickens, skin side up, in a shallow baking dish. Melt butter; add wine, salt, pepper, and tarragon and blend. Pour over chicken. Bake uncovered in a 325-degree oven for 1¼ hours, basting often with the wine sauce. Pour sauce into a small pan and heat to a boil. Add 2 tablespoons water to cornstarch, stir into sauce, and simmer, stirring constantly, until thickened. Spoon over chicken and serve. *Serves 4.*

BAKED AND FRIED CHICKEN

STUFFED CHICKEN LEGS

8 large drumsticks
¼ cup dry sherry
¼ cup chicken broth
¼ cup soy sauce
1 teaspoon garlic puree
1 tablespoon brown sugar
½ pound fresh ground pork
2 tablespoons minced onion
2 tablespoons finely chopped green pepper
⅛ teaspoon sage
½ cup flour seasoned with salt and pepper
Oil for frying
1 tablespoon cornstarch (optional)

About 2 hours before serving, remove bones and tendons from drumsticks. Combine sherry, chicken broth, soy sauce, garlic puree, and brown sugar; stir well and pour over drumsticks. Allow to marinate for 45 minutes. Meanwhile, fry pork and remove with a slotted spoon to a small dish. Pour off all but 1 tablespoon of the drippings and sauté onion and green pepper until tender. Add to pork; season with sage and mix well. Stuff into cavities of chicken legs and secure ends with small skewers. Roll chicken legs in seasoned flour and brown on all sides in oil. Remove to a shallow baking dish, pour marinade over chicken, and bake, covered, for 45 minutes at 350 degrees. Sauce may be thickened with cornstarch and ¼ cup water to make gravy. *Serves 4.*

SAN FRANCISCO BAKED CHICKEN

1 fryer, cut up
½ cup mayonnaise
1 tablespoon lemon juice
1½ tablespoons dry sherry
¾ teaspoon seasoned salt
½ teaspoon garlic salt
¼ teaspoon pepper
½ teaspoon oregano
¾ cup packaged cornflake crumbs

Wash chicken and pat dry. Combine all remaining ingredients except cornflake crumbs. Dip chicken pieces in the mayonnaise mixture, then in the crumbs, and place in a shallow baking dish. Bake uncovered at 400 degrees for 1 hour. *Serves 4.*

"SOUPER" BAKED CHICKEN

1 can condensed cream of
    mushroom soup, undiluted
¾ cup milk
1 tablespoon minced onion
1 tablespoon chopped parsley

8 meaty chicken pieces
1 cup finely crushed pack-
    aged seasoned stuffing mix
2 tablespoons melted butter

Combine ⅓ cup of the soup with ¼ cup of the milk. Add onion and parsley. Dip chicken pieces in this mixture, then roll in seasoned stuffing mix. Place in a shallow baking dish, drizzle butter over chicken, and bake uncovered at 400 degrees for 1 hour. A few minutes before chicken is done, combine remaining soup and milk and heat gently, stirring once or twice. Serve as sauce with chicken. *Serves 4.*

Fried Chicken

CHICKEN CROQUETTES

3 tablespoons butter
¼ cup flour
½ cup milk
½ cup chicken broth
1 tablespoon minced parsley
1 teaspoon lemon juice
1 teaspoon onion juice
Dash nutmeg

Dash paprika
½ teaspoon salt
Dash pepper
2 cups minced cooked
    chicken
1 cup fine dry bread crumbs
1 egg
Oil for frying

In a saucepan melt butter, stir in flour, add milk and chicken broth, and stir constantly until thick and bubbling. Add next 8 ingredients, blending well. Remove mixture to a shallow pan and refrigerate until cold. Using a scant ¼ cup for each croquette, shape 8 balls with hands wet. Roll in bread crumbs, carefully drawing croquettes out into cones. Beat egg with 2 tablespoons water and dip croquettes into egg mixture to coat, then roll again in bread crumbs. Preheat oil in a deep-fryer to 365 degrees, and fry croquettes for about 3 minutes, or until crisp and heated through. Remove to paper towels with slotted spoon. Serve topped with mushroom sauce, which can be made by heating 1 can of concentrated mushroom soup diluted with ½ cup of milk, or creamed peas prepared by following directions on package. *Serves 4.*

CRISP-FRIED CHICKEN

1 3- to 3½-pound fryer, cut up
1 egg
½ cup milk
1 cup packaged cornflake crumbs
1½ teaspoons salt
¼ teaspoon pepper
1 teaspoon paprika
1½ cups salad oil

Wash chicken pieces and pat dry. Beat together egg and milk in a shallow dish. In another dish combine cornflake crumbs and seasonings. Dip chicken pieces into egg mixture, then roll in crumb mixture. Heat oil in a heavy skillet, brown chicken lightly on one side, and turn. Reduce heat, cover, and simmer for 20 minutes, then uncover and cook 10 minutes more. *Serves 3 to 4.*

DEEP-FRIED CHICKEN

2 2-pound broilers, quartered
2 teaspoons salt
½ cup flour
4 eggs, beaten
2 cups fine dry bread crumbs
Oil for frying
Parsley sprigs

Wash chicken quarters and pat dry. Sprinkle with salt and dust with flour; dip into beaten eggs to coat completely, then roll in bread crumbs. Heat oil in deep-fryer to 350 degrees. Place chicken in one layer in fryer basket, lower into oil, and reduce heat to 325 degrees. Fry for 10 minutes, or until golden-brown. Drain on absorbent paper and serve garnished with parsley. *Serves 8.*

5

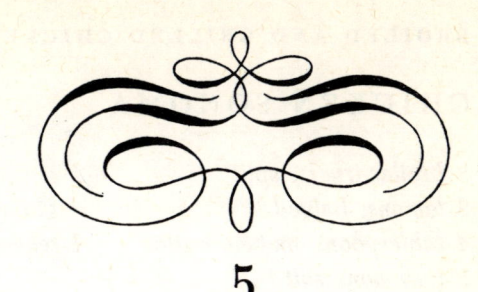

BROILED AND GRILLED CHICKEN

Broiled Chicken

FRENCH QUARTER BROILED CHICKEN

2 broiler-fryers, split
¼ cup salad oil
¼ cup Sauterne
½ teaspoon sugar
½ teaspoon monosodium glutamate
½ teaspoon paprika
¼ teaspoon salt
¼ teaspoon garlic salt
¼ teaspoon onion salt
¼ teaspoon thyme
¼ teaspoon marjoram
¼ teaspoon rosemary

Have butcher remove back and breastbones from the chicken halves and break the joints. On the day before the chickens are to be cooked, combine all the other ingredients in a jar with a tight lid, shake vigorously, and refrigerate for 24 hours. Wash chickens and pat dry. Flatten pieces by hand. Brush on marinade and place skin side down in a broiler pan. Place on rack at least 7 inches from heat and broil at 450 degrees, turning and basting every 10 minutes for 50 to 60 minutes or until tender. *Serves 4.*

CHICKEN SONOMA

2 broiler-fryers, split
2 lemons, halved
4 tablespoons melted butter
2 teaspoons salt
1 teaspoon monosodium glutamate
1 teaspoon paprika

Wash chicken halves and pat dry. Rub chickens on all sides with lemon halves, squeezing out the juice. Place, covered, in the refrigerator for 2 to 3 hours. Brush chicken with melted butter; sprinkle on all sides with seasonings and place skin side down in a large broiler pan. Broil for 8 to 10 minutes, or until golden, then turn and broil as long on the second side. Cover, remove to 325-degree oven, and bake for 35 minutes. Uncover and bake for 15 minutes more, basting once or twice with drippings. *Serves 4.*

GLAZED ROTISSERIE CHICKEN

3 tablespoons butter
1 clove garlic, crushed
1 small onion, minced
½ cup minced celery
3 tablespoons minced parsley
4 tablespoons tomato paste
1 chicken bouillon cube
1 tablespoon flour
½ cup dry sherry
½ teaspoon mixed dry herbs: savory, thyme, and basil
2 whole broilers
Salt
½ cup chicken broth

Melt butter in a small skillet. Add garlic, onion, celery, and parsley and sauté for 3 minutes. Add tomato paste and bouillon cube, stir in flour, then add sherry and herbs. Stir once more, cover, and simmer for 15 minutes. Strain.

Skewer chicken onto spit, sprinkle with salt, and place on rotisserie. Place a catch-pan beneath chicken. Begin turning chicken and brush on glaze, repeating every 10 minutes or until glaze is used up. Barbecue over coals for approximately 1 hour or until chicken is tender. Remove to a platter. Skim fat from drippings, reheat with ½ cup chicken broth, and serve with chicken. *Serves 4 to 6.*

NEW ENGLAND BARBECUED CHICKEN

1 2½- to 3-pound broiler-fryer, quartered
1 tablespoon sugar
2 teaspoons hickory-smoked salt
1 teaspoon paprika
½ teaspoon dry mustard
½ teaspoon freshly ground pepper
1 teaspoon garlic puree
3 tablespoons salad oil
½ cup dry red wine
½ cup tarragon vinegar

Place washed and dried chicken quarters on a broiler pan, skin side down. Combine all other ingredients in a jar and shake well. Brush basting sauce generously over chicken and broil 7 inches from heat for 10 minutes. Turn, baste, and broil other side for 10 minutes. Repeat, basting at each turning, until chicken has been broiled for 40 minutes or until it is tender. *Serves 4.*

ROTISSERIE INTRIGUE

1 cup mayonnaise
3 ounces dry sherry
2 teaspoons garlic puree
1 teaspoon dry mustard
1 teaspoon paprika
1 teaspoon celery salt
½ teaspoon dried rosemary
½ teaspoon poultry seasoning
½ teaspoon hickory-smoked salt
½ teaspoon sugar
2 tablespoons Worcestershire sauce
2 teaspoons bottled steak sauce
1 teaspoon tarragon vinegar
½ teaspoon Angostura bitters
¼ teaspoon Tabasco sauce
2 whole broiling chickens

Combine all ingredients except chickens and mix well. Brush marinade over chickens several hours before cooking, then refrigerate. Place chickens on a rotisserie, brush once again with sauce, and broil, continuing to baste every 5 minutes or so until they are done, approximately 1 hour. *Serves 4.*

BROILED AND GRILLED CHICKEN

LUAU DRUMSTICKS

8 chicken legs
1 8-ounce can crushed pineapple, drained
¼ cup lemon juice
¼ cup salad oil
¼ cup maple syrup
2 tablespoons soy sauce
1 teaspoon salt
¼ teaspoon pepper
¼ teaspoon ginger

Place chicken legs on a perforated broiler pan, skin side down. Combine pineapple with remaining ingredients, and brush over chicken. Broil 7 inches from heat, basting frequently, for 25 minutes on each side, or until chicken is tender. *Serves 4.*

Grilled Chicken

BARBECUED SESAME SOY CHICKEN

2 pounds chicken legs
½ cup soy sauce
1 tablespoon sugar
2 teaspoons ground ginger
2 tablespoons sesame seeds
¼ cup salad oil

Wash and dry chicken legs. Combine soy sauce, sugar, and ginger in a bowl; add chicken pieces, coat thoroughly, and marinate until time to barbecue. Toast sesame seeds in a dry skillet and set aside. Remove chicken from marinade, brush with salad oil, and grill over medium-hot coals, turning and brushing with oil occasionally, for 30 to 40 minutes or until tender. Sprinkle with toasted sesame seeds. *Serves 4 to 6.*

CALYPSO CHICKEN PLATTER

2 broiler-fryers, split
2 tablespoons salad oil
¼ cup garlic wine vinegar
1 teaspoon onion salt
Dash cayenne pepper
1 8-ounce can tomato sauce

BROILED AND GRILLED CHICKEN

Combine oil, vinegar, salt, pepper, and tomato sauce in a jar with a tight-fitting lid and shake well. Wash chicken halves and pat dry. Place chicken in a shallow pan and cover with marinade. Let stand for 1 hour, turning chicken several times. Meanwhile, prepare barbecue fire; grill chicken 5 inches from coals for about 50 minutes, turning and basting frequently. While it is cooking, prepare Spanish Rice.

SPANISH RICE:

1 8-ounce can tomato sauce with mushrooms
1 3-ounce can mushroom pieces with liquid
2 tablespoons red wine

1 6-ounce package Spanish Rice mix
2 tablespoons butter
Cherry tomatoes
Watercress

Combine tomato sauce, mushrooms, 1½ cups water, and wine in a saucepan and heat to a boil. Remove from heat, stir in Spanish Rice mix and butter, and let stand, covered, for 20 minutes. When chicken is ready, reheat very briefly, fluff with a fork, and spoon in the center of a heated platter. Surround with chicken halves and garnish with cherry tomatoes and watercress. *Serves 4.*

CHEF'S SPECIAL GRILL

2 broilers, split
½ cup chopped onion
2 tablespoons chopped capers
2 teaspoons soy sauce

2 teaspoons ground ginger
½ cup salad oil
1 cup Sauterne

Place chicken in a single layer in a dish. Combine remaining ingredients and pour over chicken. Refrigerate overnight, basting with marinade as often as possible. When coals are at the stage where they are covered with white ashes, place chicken on grill 5 inches above coals, skin side up. Grill, basting frequently, for 25 minutes, then turn and grill other side for 30 minutes or until tender, continuing to baste often. *Serves 4.*

GIDDY CHICKEN WITH GOOSEBERRY SAUCE

4 chicken breasts, split and boned
⅓ cup Cointreau
¼ cup melted butter
¼ cup olive oil
2 tablespoons lemon juice
½ teaspoon paprika
½ teaspoon salt
½ teaspoon Tabasco sauce

Wash chicken breasts and pat dry. Combine remaining ingredients for basting sauce. If chicken is to be grilled, have coals fired until they are covered with a white ash, then place chicken on a double thickness of aluminum foil and cook, basting and turning frequently, for about 35 minutes or until tender. If chicken is to be baked, place it in a dish, baste with sauce, and bake in a 325-degree oven, basting and turning every 10 minutes, for 45 minutes or until tender. Serve with sauce.

GOOSEBERRY SAUCE:

1 1-pound can gooseberries, drained
1 6-ounce jar red currant jelly
½ cup sugar
2 tablespoons Cointreau
1 teaspoon grated lemon peel
2 whole cloves

Combine ingredients in a saucepan; bring to a boil, reduce heat, and simmer for 3 minutes. *Serves 4.*

GRILLED PECAN-STUFFED CHICKEN BREASTS

4 whole chicken breasts
3 tablespoons lemon juice
6 tablespoons melted butter
3 cups toasted shredded bread
¾ cup chopped pecans
½ cup chopped celery
¼ cup chopped onion
2 teaspoons salt
¼ teaspoon pepper

Brush chicken with lemon juice, then with 2 tablespoons melted butter. Place shredded bread into a mixing bowl; pour on 4 tablespoons melted butter and ¼ cup hot water. Add pecans, celery, onion, salt, and pepper and toss well. Prepare 4 double-thick squares of aluminum foil, 12 x 12 inches. Divide dressing into 4 mounds on the foil, place a chicken breast over each mound, and seal packets tightly. Grill over charcoal for 40 minutes or until tender. Chicken breasts may also be baked at 400 degrees for 40 minutes. *Serves 4.*

POLYNESIAN CHICKEN ON A SPIT

1 large roasting chicken
½ cup MJB White & Wild Rice Mix
½ pound lean ground lamb
1 egg, beaten
¼ cup minced onion
¼ cup minced celery
¼ cup minced mushrooms
¼ cup minced parsley
¼ cup slivered almonds
5 ounces (1¼ sticks) butter
1 cup chicken broth
2 teaspoons salt
Dash freshly ground pepper
Dash nutmeg
Dash thyme
Dash crumbled rosemary
Grated orange rind

Prepare charcoal fire; chicken is ready to cook when coals are covered with white ashes. Wash and dry chicken. Cook rice in salted water to cover for 7 minutes, and drain. In a bowl combine rice with the next 7 ingredients in the order listed. Melt ¼ stick butter in chicken broth; add to mixture. Add next 5 ingredients, toss lightly, and spoon into chicken cavities. Close openings, truss, and balance evenly on spit. Cook for 1½ hours, basting often with remaining stick of butter, which has been melted and seasoned with grated orange rind. *Serves 4 to 6.*

6
ROASTS WITH STUFFINGS

THE COMPLETE CAPON DINNER

½ cup chopped celery
½ cup chopped onion
½ cup chopped pitted ripe olives
½ cup chopped walnuts
1 cup chopped, pared apple
1 8-ounce package seasoned stuffing mix
½ teaspoon poultry seasoning
Seasoned salt
1 6- to 8-pound fresh capon

Salt
Pepper
Melted butter
8 medium potatoes
8 tiny white onions
½ pound fresh mushrooms
Paprika
2 1-pound cans whole baby carrots
Flour

On the night before serving, combine first 5 ingredients in a bowl; cover and refrigerate. Four hours before serving, prepare stuffing mix according to package directions and add refrigerated mixture. Add poultry seasoning and seasoned salt to taste. Rub cavities of capon with salt and pepper, spoon in stuffing, and close openings

ROASTS WITH STUFFINGS

with skewers. Tie drumsticks together and place capon, breast side up, in a roasting pan. Brush with melted butter, then cover loosely with aluminum foil. Roast for 3 hours in a 350-degree oven, basting frequently with pan drippings.

Meanwhile, pare potatoes and peel onions. Place in a bowl, cover with water, and refrigerate. Wash and remove stems from mushrooms and set aside. Just before the last hour of roasting, dry potatoes and onions and brush with melted butter, then sprinkle on paprika. Arrange potatoes around capon and continue roasting, uncovered. About 20 minutes before end of roasting time, partially insert toothpicks into onions and stick them in a line along the center of the capon's breastbone. Partially drain carrots and heat in a saucepan. Sauté mushrooms in melted butter until tender; keep carrots and mushrooms warm.

When capon, potatoes, and onions are done, remove them to a large hot platter and keep warm. Make gravy from drippings in roasting pan, thickening with a paste made of flour and 2 tablespoons water. Drain carrots, drizzle melted butter on top, and place on the heated platter along with the capon, potatoes, and onions. Remove skewers from capon, add mushrooms, and serve platter along with gravy. *Serves 8.*

ROAST CHICKEN WITH NUT STUFFING

2 cups dry bread crumbs
6 tablespoons butter
¼ cup seedless raisins
¼ cup currants
2 tablespoons chopped walnuts
2 tablespoons chopped hazelnuts
2 tablespoons chopped pine nuts

2 tablespoons chopped almonds
¼ cup sugar
1 cup chicken stock
2 teaspoons salt
¼ teaspoon pepper
1 large roasting chicken

Sauté bread crumbs in 4 tablespoons butter for 5 minutes, **stirring occasionally**. Add raisins, currants, nuts, sugar, and ½ cup chicken stock. Mix well and set aside. Mix salt and pepper and rub on chicken inside and out. Place nut stuffing in cavities and close with skewers. Melt 2 tablespoons butter; brush on chicken and roast in a 350-degree oven for 2½ hours. Add remaining ½ cup chicken stock after first hour; use drippings for basting and gravy. *Serves 6.*

SHANGHAI CAPON

1 7- to 8-pound capon
1 pound thin egg noodles
4 ounces (1 stick) butter
1 cup sliced fresh mushrooms
1 4¾-ounce can pâté de foie
1 tablespoon soy sauce

Place capon on a wire rack over boiling water in a large saucepan. Cover tightly and steam until tender, about 1½ hours. Meanwhile cook noodles in salted water until tender; drain well and cool. When chicken is done, allow it to cool so it may be handled. Cut all along breast, laying back the skin and meat, and remove breastbone. Melt butter in a large skillet, reserving 1 tablespoon, and sauté mushrooms for 5 minutes, then add noodles, pâté, and soy sauce and toss well. Fill chicken cavity with noodle stuffing, folding meat and skin back into place, and secure with toothpicks. Brush with reserved melted butter and heat uncovered in a shallow baking dish in a 325-degree oven for ½ hour. Meanwhile, prepare cheese sauce.

CHEESE SAUCE:

2 tablespoons butter
2 tablespoons flour
1 cup half and half
1 cup chicken broth
1 cup grated Cheddar cheese

Melt butter, stir in flour, then add half and half and broth, stirring until bubbling. Add Cheddar cheese and stir until it melts. When chicken has finished baking, pour sauce over it and heat 5 minutes more. *Serves 8.*

ROASTS WITH STUFFINGS

CRAB-STUFFED CHICKEN HALVES

2 2- to 2½-pound broilers, split
½ teaspoon garlic salt
¼ cup melted butter
¼ cup dry sherry
¼ teaspoon paprika

Wash and dry chicken halves and sprinkle with garlic salt. Combine melted butter, sherry, and paprika and keep warm. Place chicken skin side up in a single layer in a shallow baking pan, and brush some of the sherry mixture over it. Roast for 45 minutes at 350 degrees, basting often. Remove and let cool in the pan while preparing stuffing.

CRAB STUFFING:

¼ cup milk
1½ cups prepared packaged stuffing mix
2 6½-ounce cans crab meat, drained
¼ cup melted butter
1 teaspoon prepared mustard
¼ teaspoon cayenne pepper

Pour milk over stuffing mix and toss until bread cubes are moistened. Break crab meat into small bits and add to stuffing. Heat butter, mustard, and cayenne pepper together and add; toss stuffing. Turn chicken halves skin side down and spoon stuffing into depressions. Return to 350-degree oven for 30 minutes, basting now and then with leftover basting liquid or pan drippings. Serves 4.

ROAST CHICKEN WITH MEAT-RICE STUFFING

1 pound ground beef
3 tablespoons olive oil
½ cup half-cooked long-grain white rice
¼ cup pine nuts
3 teaspoons salt
1 teaspoon pepper
¼ teaspoon nutmeg
¼ teaspoon thyme
1 6-pound roasting chicken
1 medium onion, quartered
1 stalk celery
½ cup melted butter

Sauté ground beef in olive oil for 10 minutes. Add rice, pine nuts, 1 teaspoon salt, ½ teaspoon pepper, nutmeg, and thyme, mixing well. Put this stuffing into the chicken and sew openings carefully. Place in a deep saucepan with 2 quarts water, 2 teaspoons salt, ½ teaspoon pepper, onion, and celery. Cover and simmer for 1½ hours. Remove chicken and drain. Place in a roasting pan and brush with melted butter. Roast at 400 degrees for 30 minutes, or until well browned. *Serves 6.*

Stuffings

CABBAGE STUFFING

6 cups shredded cabbage
¼ cup chopped onion
2 teaspoons caraway seeds
1 teaspoon salt
¼ teaspoon pepper
2 eggs
¼ cup milk

Cook cabbage with 1 cup water in a covered saucepan for 5 minutes. Drain. Add onion, caraway seeds, salt, and pepper. Beat together eggs and milk and pour over cabbage; toss well. Place stuffing in chicken cavities. *Makes enough for a 5- to 6-pound chicken.*

CORN STUFFING

1 16-ounce can creamed corn
3 tablespoons chopped green pepper
3 tablespoons chopped onion
3 tablespoons melted butter
2 eggs, beaten
1½ teaspoons salt
4 cups shredded fresh white bread, with crusts removed

Combine all ingredients and toss lightly. Place stuffing in chicken cavities. *Makes enough for a 6-pound chicken.*

INDIAN STUFFING

¼ cup pine nuts
5 tablespoons butter
1 cup uncooked long-grain white rice
1 chicken liver, chopped
¼ cup currants
2 teaspoons salt
¼ teaspoon pepper

Toast pine nuts in 1 tablespoon butter in a large skillet until they turn light pink. Remove and set aside. Add 2 tablespoons butter to skillet, and toast rice and chicken livers over low heat until rice is lightly browned. Return pine nuts to rice and add currants, salt and pepper, and 2½ cups boiling water. Simmer over low heat, uncovered, for 20 minutes or until liquid has been absorbed and rice is tender. Stir in 2 tablespoons butter and spoon into chicken. *Makes enough for a 5- to 6-pound chicken.*

MEAT MIXTURE STUFFING

¼ pound chicken livers, chopped
½ pound fresh mushrooms, sliced
6 tablespoons butter
6 slices bacon
4 cups soft bread cubes
½ pound ground ham
½ teaspoon salt
½ teaspoon sage
Dash nutmeg
½ teaspoon garlic puree
3 tablespoons dry sherry

Sauté chicken livers and mushrooms in 3 tablespoons butter for 5 minutes, then remove. Fry bacon in the same pan until crisp; drain and crumble. In a bowl combine bread cubes, chicken liver and mushroom mixture, bacon, ham, and seasonings. Melt 2 tablespoons butter in ¼ cup water and add. Toss and place in chicken cavities. Refrigerate stuffing separately from chicken if made before chicken is ready to be roasted. Melt garlic puree and 1 tablespoon butter together and brush on chicken. Baste with dry sherry several times while roasting. *Makes enough for a 5- to 6-pound chicken.*

RAW POTATO STUFFING

2 medium onions
4 ounces (1 stick) butter
½ cup minced parsley
6 medium potatoes

2 stalks celery
2 teaspoons salt
¼ teaspoon pepper

Chop 1 onion. Melt butter in a skillet and sauté chopped onion and parsley for 3 minutes, then set aside. Pare potatoes and cut into chunks. Remove strings from celery and cut into chunks; peel and quarter remaining onion. Combine potatoes, celery, and quartered onion and run through a food grinder. Add sautéed vegetables, salt, and pepper and mix well. Spoon into chicken. *Makes enough for a 5- to 6-pound chicken.*

SAUSAGE-APPLE STUFFING

1 pound fresh pork
  sausage meat
1 tablespoon minced onion
  flakes

1 cup chopped tart apple
2 cups dry bread crumbs
1 teaspoon salt
Dash pepper

Fry pork sausage lightly with onion flakes and remove all but 2 tablespoons of the drippings. Combine with ½ cup hot water and remaining ingredients. *Makes enough for a 4- to 5-pound chicken.*

SCANDINAVIAN STUFFING

3½ cups shredded soft white
  bread
1½ cups chopped apple
½ cup seedless raisins
2 tablespoons butter

½ teaspoon grated lemon
  peel
¼ teaspoon cinnamon
½ teaspoon salt
1 teaspoon lemon juice

Combine all ingredients in order listed; add ¼ cup water and toss well. Spoon into chicken cavities. *Makes enough for a 5-pound chicken.*

ROASTS WITH STUFFINGS

WILD RICE STUFFING

1 cup uncooked wild rice
½ cup minced onion
1 cup minced celery
1 tablespoon minced parsley
1 tablespoon minced chives

1 teaspoon salt
¼ teaspoon pepper
Pinch poultry seasoning
2 tablespoons melted butter

Rinse rice thoroughly in cold water. Bring 2 cups water to a boil, add rice, cover, and cook for 20 minutes. Drain and place over low heat, covered, for 5 minutes; do not stir. Add remaining ingredients in the order listed, toss, and spoon into chicken. *Makes enough for a 4- to 5-pound chicken.*

MUSHROOM-HERB STUFFING

½ cup finely chopped green onions
2½ cups coarsely chopped fresh mushrooms
4 ounces (1 stick) butter or margarine
2 cups packaged herb stuffing mix

¼ cup minced parsley
1 teaspoon dried marjoram
¼ teaspoon poultry seasoning
¼ teaspoon nutmeg
1 teaspoon salt
Dash pepper

Sauté onions and mushrooms in butter for 5 minutes. Add to stuffing mix. Add seasonings, toss lightly, and spoon into chicken cavities. *Makes enough for a 5- to 6-pound chicken.*

OYSTER STUFFING

1 pint oysters
2 tablespoons minced onion
4 tablespoons butter
5 cups shredded fresh white bread, with crusts removed
¼ cup minced parsley

¼ cup chopped celery
2 eggs, slightly beaten
1 teaspoon salt
½ teaspoon paprika
Dash nutmeg
¼ cup milk

Drain and chop oysters, reserving ¼ cup oyster liquor. Sauté onion in butter until limp. Add to shredded bread, then add all the remaining ingredients. If a moister dressing is desired, add more oyster liquor. *Makes enough for a 5-pound chicken.*

ISLAND STUFFING

4 cups dry bread cubes
¾ cup finely chopped green pepper
¾ cup well-drained pineapple tidbits
½ cup finely chopped walnuts
¾ cup finely chopped celery
1½ teaspoons salt
1 teaspoon paprika
Dash cayenne pepper
¼ cup melted butter
2 eggs

Combine all ingredients except butter and eggs. Lightly stir whole eggs into the butter, pour over stuffing and mix well. Spoon into chicken cavities. *Makes enough for a 5- to 6-pound chicken.*

CORNBREAD-WALNUT STUFFING

½ cup chopped onion
½ cup chopped celery
4 ounces (1 stick) butter or margarine
2 cups packaged cornbread stuffing
1 cup lightly toasted white bread cubes
1 cup chopped walnuts
1 teaspoon salt
¼ teaspoon pepper
½ teaspoon monosodium glutamate
½ teaspoon poultry seasoning
¼ teaspoon thyme
2 eggs, slightly beaten

Sauté onion and celery in butter for 5 minutes. Combine stuffing, bread cubes, walnuts, and seasonings in a large bowl. Add eggs and ½ cup water and toss. *Makes enough for a 5-pound chicken.*

7

STEWS

CHICKEN FRICASSEE

1 4-pound stewing chicken, cut up
3½ teaspoons salt
¼ teaspoon poultry seasoning
6 peppercorns
1 small onion, peeled
1 stalk celery

1 1⅜-ounce package dried cream of leek soup mix
1 10-ounce package frozen peas with onions
1 cup light cream
1 8-ounce package broad egg noodles

Place chicken, 3 teaspoons salt, poultry seasoning, peppercorns, onion, and celery in a large saucepan and barely cover with water. Bring to a boil, cover, and simmer until tender. Drain, reserving liquid. Remove skin and bones from chicken and cut into bite-sized pieces. In a large saucepan combine soup mix with 1½ cups reserved chicken broth. Add frozen peas with onions, bring to a boil, then reduce heat and stir in ½ teaspoon salt and cream. Cover and keep warm over very low flame. Meanwhile, prepare noodles according to package directions. Add chicken to sauce and heat while noodles are cooking. Drain noodles and serve chicken on top. *Serves 4 to 5.*

STEWS

CHICKEN FRICASSEE WITH MEATBALLS

3 pounds meaty chicken pieces
4 tablespoons butter
1 cup chopped onion
¼ cup chopped parsley
¼ cup flour

3 cups chicken broth
1½ teaspoons salt
½ teaspoon garlic salt
¼ teaspoon freshly ground pepper
1 teaspoon crumbled rosemary

In a large Dutch oven brown chicken pieces in butter, then remove. Sauté onion and parsley in drippings for 3 minutes; stir in flour and blend in chicken broth. Season with remaining ingredients and return chicken to sauce. Bring to a boil, reduce heat, and simmer, covered, for 30 minutes. Meanwhile, make meatballs.

MEATBALLS:

1 pound ground beef
1 egg, beaten
2 tablespoons milk

½ cup fine dry bread crumbs
½ teaspoon salt
¼ teaspoon thyme

Combine all ingredients, mixing well. Shape into 1-inch balls, add to chicken, and simmer for 30 minutes more. *Serves 6.*

CHICKEN STEWED IN BEER

1 5- to 6-pound chicken
½ lemon
3 teaspoons salt
1 cup sliced celery
1 cup chopped onion
¼ cup chopped parsley
1 clove garlic, chopped
2 cups beer

6 carrots, cut in 2-inch pieces
18 small new potatoes, peeled
18 small white onions, peeled
24 small fresh button mushrooms
1 10-ounce package frozen peas

Rub chicken inside and out with lemon, releasing juice as you go. Sprinkle inside and out with 1 teaspoon salt. Place in a large kettle with celery, chopped onion, parsley, garlic, and 2 teaspoons salt. Pour beer on top, bring to a boil, cover, and reduce heat to simmer. Cook for 1½ hours, or until chicken is almost tender. Add carrots, potatoes, white onions, and mushrooms, and simmer 20 minutes more. Add peas and simmer 10 minutes. Remove chicken from broth, cut into serving pieces, and place in soup bowls. Ladle vegetables and broth over chicken. *Serves 6.*

STUFFED CHICKEN AND VEGETABLE STEW

4 medium onions
6 tomatoes
½ pound ground lean pork
1 teaspoon salt
½ teaspoon pepper
4 tablespoons chopped mustard pickles
1 tablespoon minced capers
½ cup bread crumbs
2 eggs, beaten

1 large roasting chicken
4 tablespoons butter
1 bay leaf, crushed
3 medium potatoes, peeled and cubed
6 carrots, quartered
1 cup chicken broth
2 tablespoons flour
½ cup cooking sherry

Mince 2 onions and 2 tomatoes. Combine thoroughly with next 7 ingredients and stuff into cavities of chicken; close openings with skewers. Slice remaining 2 onions and quarter the 4 tomatoes. Heat butter in a deep kettle and brown onion slices and chicken together until meat is golden on all sides. Add tomatoes and bay leaf. Cover and simmer for 2 hours, turning chicken occasionally. Add potatoes, carrots, and chicken broth and continue cooking for ½ hour.

Remove chicken onto a warm platter, surround with vegetables, and keep warm. Strain stock and return to kettle, thickening if necessary with a paste made of flour and 2 tablespoons of water. Add sherry and bring to a quick boil. Serve with chicken in a separate bowl. *Serves 6.*

STEWS

PEASANT DINNER

- 1 2- to 2½-pound fryer, cut up, with giblets
- 4 tablespoons butter
- 2 pounds beef short ribs
- 4 14-ounce cans chicken broth
- 1 beef marrow bone
- 6 cloves
- 1 bay leaf
- 1 teaspoon salt
- ¼ teaspoon pepper
- 1 cup thinly sliced carrot strips
- 1 cup thinly sliced turnip strips
- 1 cup diagonally sliced celery
- ½ cup sliced leeks
- 2 cups coarsely shredded cabbage
- ½ cup medium egg noodles

Brown chicken pieces lightly on all sides in butter and place in a 6-quart saucepan. Add short ribs, chicken broth, and 1 soup can water and bring to a boil. Meanwhile, combine in a piece of cheesecloth the chicken giblets, marrow bone, cloves, and bay leaf. Tie securely and add to meat. Add salt, pepper, carrot strips, turnip strips, celery, and leeks, and simmer uncovered for 1½ hours. Remove cheesecloth container and add cabbage and noodles. Simmer ½ hour more. Place pieces of meat in large soup bowls and spoon vegetables and broth over them. Can be served with tossed salad and buttered French bread. *Serves 6.*

SOUTHERN CHICKEN STEW

- 1 5-pound stewing chicken, cut up
- 1 pound bottom round beef, cubed
- 3 medium onions, quartered
- 2 tablespoons salt
- ½ teaspoon pepper
- 6 sprigs parsley
- 1 10-ounce package frozen lima beans
- 3 tablespoons catsup
- 1 10-ounce package frozen okra
- 3 medium potatoes, peeled and cubed
- 2 stalks celery, sliced
- 2 fresh tomatoes, chopped
- 1 cup drained kernel corn
- 4 tablespoons butter
- 2 tablespoons sugar
- 2 tablespoons vinegar
- Dash cayenne pepper

In a large saucepan combine cleaned chicken pieces, beef cubes, 2 quarts water, onions, salt, pepper, and parsley. Simmer covered for 2½ hours, then remove meat and set aside. Strain broth. Add lima beans, okra, potatoes, catsup, celery, tomatoes, corn, and butter to broth. Simmer covered for ½ hour, stirring occasionally. Meanwhile, remove chicken from bones and cut into cubes. Add meat to broth and cook, uncovered, until almost all of the liquid is absorbed. Add sugar, vinegar, and cayenne pepper and cook for 5 minutes more. *Serves 6.*

OLD-FASHIONED CHICKEN STEW WITH DUMPLINGS

2 fryers, cut up, with giblets
½ teaspoon Bouquet Garni
3 teaspoons salt
½ cup Dixie Fry
½ cup salad oil
½ pound fresh mushrooms, sliced
1 1-pound can stewed tomatoes
3 carrots, cut diagonally into slices
3 stalks celery, cut diagonally into slices
12 pearl onions, peeled
¼ teaspoon pepper
¼ teaspoon basil
¼ teaspoon thyme
¼ teaspoon marjoram
1 10-ounce package frozen or 2 cups fresh peas
½ cup Burgundy
2 tablespoons flour
2 cups Bisquick
¾ cup milk
2 tablespoons parsley flakes

Early in the day, place giblets, neck, and back pieces in a saucepan with Bouquet Garni, 1 teaspoon salt, and 3 cups water. Cover and simmer 1 hour, then strain out broth and set aside for later use. Meanwhile, shake remaining chicken pieces with Dixie Fry in a paper bag and brown on all sides in oil. Remove and drain. In the same oil, sauté mushrooms for 5 minutes, remove, and set aside. Return chicken to pan, and add chicken broth, tomatoes, carrots, celery, onions, 2 teaspoons salt, pepper, basil, thyme, and marjoram. Cover and simmer for 45 minutes, then let cool and skim off fat.

STEWS

One-half hour before serving, reheat chicken. Add peas, mushrooms, and burgundy; cover and cook for 15 minutes. Make a paste of flour and 2 tablespoons of water and stir into juices to thicken to gravy consistency. Combine biscuit mix with milk and parsley, drop by spoonful on the stew, and cook uncovered over low heat for 10 minutes. *Serves 6.*

PAISANO STEW WITH POLENTA

4 *tablespoons butter*
2 *tablespoons olive oil*
5 *pounds chicken parts*
1 *medium onion, thinly sliced*
1 *clove garlic, minced*
2 *teaspoons salt*
5 *whole cloves*

5 *whole allspice*
1 *bay leaf*
¼ *teaspoon crushed rosemary*
¼ *teaspoon thyme*
1 *16-ounce can Italian plum tomatoes, undrained*
1 *cup red wine*

Heat butter and oil together in a large Dutch oven and brown chicken pieces, a few at a time, on both sides. Set aside. In remaining drippings sauté onion and garlic for 5 minutes. Return chicken to pot and add all remaining ingredients. Cover and simmer for 1½ hours, or until chicken is tender. About ½ hour before chicken is done, prepare polenta.

POLENTA:

1½ *cups yellow cornmeal*   2 *teaspoons salt*

Place cornmeal and 1½ teaspoons salt in a medium-sized bowl. Add 1 cup water and stir until well blended. Bring 4½ more cups of water and remaining ½ teaspoon salt to a boil in a large saucepan and gradually stir in cornmeal mixture. Continue to stir over low heat until mixture is smooth, then cook over very low heat without stirring for about 20 minutes, or until a crust forms around the edge. Remove from heat, run a knife around the edge, and invert onto a platter. Surround with chicken pieces and cover with sauce. *Serves 6.*

CHICKEN GUMBO

2 teaspoons salt
1 teaspoon pepper
1 teaspoon garlic puree
1 5-pound stewing chicken, cut up
2 medium onions, chopped
4 tablespoons butter
½ pound boiled ham, cubed
½ teaspoon thyme
½ teaspoon rosemary
¼ teaspoon ground chili peppers
1 cup canned peeled tomatoes
1 10-ounce package frozen okra
24 oysters
2 tablespoons cornstarch
Hot cooked white rice

Combine salt, pepper, and garlic puree and rub into washed chicken pieces. Sauté chicken and onions in butter in a large skillet until brown on all sides. Add ham, 1 quart water, thyme, rosemary, chili peppers, and tomatoes. Cook covered over low heat for 1½ hours. Add okra and cook 15 minutes more, then add oysters and continue cooking for 5 minutes, or until heated through. Dissolve cornstarch in ¼ cup cold water, stir into stew, and mix well. When thickened, serve immediately over hot rice. *Serves 6.*

8
CASSEROLES

CHICKEN CASSEROLE ALSACE

¼ pound dried mushrooms
2 2- to 2½-pound chickens, cut up, not including backs and wings
¼ cup olive oil
4 tablespoons butter
½ cup minced celery
½ cup minced onion
½ cup tomato juice
1 teaspoon salt
¼ teaspoon pepper
1 bay leaf, crumbled
½ cup sour cream
1 10-ounce package frozen mixed vegetables, thawed
1 cup Rhine wine

Early in the day soak dried mushrooms in water to barely cover; let stand for several hours. About 1¼ hours before serving, brown chickens in olive oil in a large ovenproof skillet. Reduce heat and simmer uncovered for 30 minutes. Meanwhile, in another pan, melt butter and sauté celery, onion, and drained mushrooms. Add tomato juice and seasonings, cover, and simmer for 30 minutes. Add sour cream to sauce and add vegetables to chicken. When both are warm, pour sauce over chicken. Add wine, cover, and bake at 325 degrees for 20 minutes. *Serves 6.*

CASSEROLES

CHICKEN CLAMBAKE

- 6 chicken thighs, skinned
- 3 tablespoons butter
- 6 to 8 small white onions, peeled
- 2 7½-ounce cans minced clams
- ¼ cup flour
- 1 teaspoon salt
- ¼ teaspoon freshly ground pepper
- 1 teaspoon poultry seasoning
- 1 10-ounce package frozen peas and carrots, thawed
- 12 unbaked prepared baking powder biscuits

Sauté chicken thighs in butter on both sides over low heat for 30 minutes. Meanwhile, cook onions in 1 cup boiling water for 5 minutes. Drain and reserve broth. Drain clams, reserving liquor. When chicken is done, remove from pan and stir flour, salt, pepper, and poultry seasoning into pan drippings. Blend in onion broth and clam juice and heat to a boil, stirring until slightly thickened. Remove from heat and place chicken, onions, clams, peas and carrots, and sauce in a baking dish in that order. Place biscuits on top and bake uncovered at 400 degrees for 15 minutes, or until biscuits are well browned. *Serves 6.*

AMERICAN-STYLE CHICKEN RISOTTO

- 2 tablespoons butter
- 1 cup uncooked long-grain white rice
- 2 small fryers, cut up
- 4 tablespoons flour
- 4 tablespoons olive oil
- 1 clove garlic, minced
- ½ cup chopped onion
- Tiny pinch powdered saffron
- 1 tablespoon salt
- 2 14-ounce cans chicken broth
- ½ cup grated Parmesan cheese
- 2 tablespoons finely minced parsley

In a large skillet melt butter, spread rice, and brown over low flame. Remove from pan and reserve. Remove skin from chicken pieces and shake with flour in a clean paper bag. Heat oil in same skillet and brown chicken, a few pieces at a time, until all are done; set aside. Sauté garlic and onion in remaining drippings, then add rice, saffron, salt, and chicken broth and mix well. Pour into a shallow baking dish, place chicken on top, and cover. Bake at 350 degrees for 1 hour or until rice is tender and liquid is absorbed. Remove cover, sprinkle on Parmesan cheese and parsley, heat 5 minutes more, and serve. *Serves 6.*

FRENCH CHICKEN CASSEROLE WITH DUMPLINGS

2 3-pound fryers, cut up	1 clove garlic, minced
1 tablespoon salt	½ teaspoon marjoram
1 teaspoon pepper	¼ teaspoon thyme
4 ounces (1 stick) butter	4 sprigs parsley
2 cloves	1 bay leaf
12 small white onions	1¼ cups white wine
12 mushrooms	½ teaspoon saffron
3 carrots, peeled and sliced	½ pint sour cream

Rub chicken pieces with salt and pepper. Melt butter in a flameproof casserole and brown chicken on all sides. Place cloves in one of the onions and add to chicken with remaining onions and next 8 ingredients. Cover and bake at 375 degrees for 1 hour, then remove from oven and place over low heat on stove. Discard onion with cloves. Dissolve saffron in 2 tablespoons hot water and add to chicken. Gently stir in sour cream.

DUMPLINGS:

1½ cups sifted flour	2 eggs, beaten
1 tablespoon baking powder	⅓ cup milk
1 teaspoon salt	

Sift together flour, baking powder, and salt. Stir in eggs and milk and blend into a smooth batter. When casserole is boiling, drop batter by teaspoonsful around the perimeter. Cover and cook over low heat for 15 minutes; do not open lid while dumplings are cooking. *Serves 6.*

CHICKEN TAMALE PIE

½ cup dry yellow cornmeal
3¼ teaspoons salt
3 cups sliced cooked chicken
1 cup chopped onion
1 clove garlic, minced
2 tablespoons butter or oil
1 tablespoon chili powder
1 1-pound can peeled, whole tomatoes
1 8-ounce can ripe pitted olives, drained
1 8-ounce can cream-style corn
¾ cup grated Parmesan cheese

Cook cornmeal in 3 cups boiling water and 1¼ teaspoons salt, stirring frequently, for 10 minutes or until thick. Spread in a buttered oblong baking dish and place chicken over cornmeal. Sauté onion and garlic in butter until tender, add 2 teaspoons salt and all other ingredients except cheese, and simmer for 5 minutes. Pour sauce over chicken. Sprinkle on Parmesan cheese and bake uncovered at 350 degrees for 40 minutes. *Serves 6 to 8.*

INDIVIDUAL CHICKEN SOUFFLÉS

½ cup chopped mushrooms
2 tablespoons chopped green onion
3 tablespoons butter
½ teaspoon salt
Dash paprika
Dash nutmeg
3 tablespoons flour
1 cup warm milk
5 eggs, separated
2 cups minced cooked chicken

In a medium-sized saucepan, sauté mushrooms and onion in butter until tender. Season with salt, paprika, and nutmeg. Add flour and stir until well blended; add warm milk, heat, and stir until bubbling and thick. Lightly beat egg yolks; add with chicken. Heat, stirring, for 1 minute, and allow mixture to cool. Beat egg whites until stiff and gently fold into chicken mixture. Butter 8 individual 8-ounce soufflé dishes or custard cups, fill each three-quarters full, and place on a baking sheet; bake at 350 degrees for 25 minutes. *Serves 8.*

CHICKEN MORNAY *EN CASSEROLE*

2 10-ounce packages frozen chopped broccoli
11 tablespoons butter
¼ cup light cream
3 teaspoons salt
Dash nutmeg
2 tablespoons minced onion
6 tablespoons flour
3 cups milk
½ cup grated Gruyère cheese
¾ cup grated Parmesan cheese
Dash cayenne pepper
4 cups ground cooked chicken

Prepare broccoli according to package directions; when very tender, drain well. Press through a sieve, add 3 tablespoons butter, cream, 2 teaspoons salt, and nutmeg. Place in a small saucepan and set aside for later use. Melt 6 tablespoons butter in a heavy saucepan over low heat. Add onion and sauté for 3 minutes. Stir in flour, then gradually add milk, stirring constantly until smooth and thickened. Add Gruyère cheese, ½ cup grated Parmesan cheese, 1 teaspoon salt, and cayenne pepper, and stir until cheese has melted. Remove from heat. Reserve ½ cup of sauce. Add chicken to remaining sauce and mix well. Butter 4 individual casseroles, divide chicken mixture among them, and pour a little of the reserved sauce over each, then sprinkle 1 tablespoon Parmesan cheese and ½ tablespoon butter on each casserole and place under broiler until lightly browned. Keep warm. Reheat broccoli; using a pastry tube, garnish perimeter of each casserole with creamed broccoli and serve immediately. *Serves 4.*

DOUBLE-CRUST CHICKEN PIE

PASTRY:

1⅔ cups sifted flour
¼ cup grated Parmesan cheese
½ teaspoon salt
4 ounces (1 stick) butter or margarine

Sift flour and salt, and blend in Parmesan cheese with a fork. Blend in shortening until crumbly, then add ¼ cup ice water, 1

CASSEROLES

tablespoon at a time, adding more if necessary, until dough holds together. Divide dough in half and roll into balls; wrap in waxed paper and chill until 1 hour before serving, then roll out the balls into two 11-inch circles and place one in a 9-inch pie plate.

FILLING:

6 slices bacon
3 cups bite-sized pieces of cooked chicken
1 can condensed mushroom soup, undiluted
4 hard-cooked eggs, sliced

Fry and drain bacon and cut into 2-inch pieces. Spread chicken as first layer in pie and pour half the soup over it, then arrange bacon and eggs as second layer and top with remaining soup. Place second pastry round over the top; seal and flute edges and cut several slits in the top. Place in a 425-degree oven and bake for 35-40 minutes. Let cool for 5 minutes. *Serves 6.*

- CHICKEN-VEGETABLE CASSEROLE

2½ pounds meaty chicken pieces (no backs or wings)
¼ cup olive oil
1 4-ounce can mushroom pieces, drained
1 small onion, minced
2 stalks celery, minced
2 tablespoons minced parsley
4 tablespoons butter
½ cup tomato juice
1 teaspoon salt
¼ teaspoon pepper
¼ teaspoon oregano
1 small bay leaf, crushed
½ cup sour cream
1 10-ounce package frozen mixed vegetables
1 cup Sauterne

Brown chicken pieces in olive oil on all sides. Reduce heat and cook uncovered for 30 minutes. Meanwhile, in a small skillet, sauté mushrooms, onion, celery, and parsley in butter until tender. Add tomato juice and seasonings, cover, and simmer for 25 minutes. Stir in Sauterne and sour cream and heat gently. Cook frozen vegetables according to package directions and drain. When all is ready, place chicken pieces in a baking dish, add vegetables, and top with sauce. Cover and bake at 350 degrees for 20 minutes. *Serves 4.*

MINUTE CHICKEN PIE

1 can condensed cream of chicken soup, undiluted
¼ cup milk
Dash nutmeg
½ teaspoon crushed bay leaf
2 tablespoons chopped pimiento
1 8-ounce can small white onions, drained
1 8-ounce can peas and carrots, drained
1 cup diced cooked chicken (or use canned)
1 8-ounce tube prepared biscuit dough

Combine soup with milk. Add all remaining ingredients except biscuit dough, then pour into a 1½ quart casserole and bake uncovered at 375 degrees for 20 minutes. Remove from oven, place rounds of biscuit dough around edge of chicken, and bake according to directions on tube. *Serves 4.*

CHICKEN TETRAZZINI

2 fryers, cut up
2½ cups fine spaghetti, broken into 1½-inch lengths
1 large onion, chopped
2 tablespoons butter
1 can concentrated cream of chicken soup, undiluted
1 13-ounce can evaporated milk
1 4-ounce can sliced mushrooms with liquid
2½ cups grated sharp Cheddar cheese
¼ cup grated Parmesan cheese

Stew chickens until tender, following instructions on page 10. Remove skin and bones, break into bite-sized pieces, and place in a shallow buttered baking dish. Cook spaghetti in 1½ quarts boiling salted water until barely tender; rinse and drain, then set aside. Sauté onion in butter until clear. Stir in cream of chicken soup and evaporated milk; add mushrooms with their liquid and heat through. Stir in spaghetti, remove from heat, and pour over chicken. Sprinkle first with Cheddar cheese, then with Parmesan, and bake uncovered at 350 degrees for 30 minutes. *Serves 8.*

CASSEROLES

CHICKEN UNDER A BLANKET

3 cups sliced cooked chicken
4 teaspoons salt
½ teaspoon pepper
3 tablespoons minced parsley
1½ cups sifted flour
½ teaspoon baking powder
1 egg, beaten
2 cups milk

Place chicken in a buttered baking dish and sprinkle on 2 teaspoons salt, pepper, and parsley. Sift flour, baking powder, and 2 teaspoons salt together into a bowl; stir in egg and milk and beat until smooth. Pour the batter over the chicken and cook casserole, uncovered, in a 350-degree oven for 1 hour. *Serves 6.*

HOSTESS'S FAVORITE CASSEROLE

1 5-pound chicken
1 12-ounce package medium-wide noodles
1 can condensed cream of mushroom soup, undiluted
1 medium onion, chopped
1 green pepper, seeded and chopped
1 4-ounce can sliced mushrooms, drained
2 tablespoons minced pimiento
1 teaspoon salt
½ teaspoon celery salt
¼ teaspoon pepper
2 cups diced cooked ham
1 10-ounce package frozen peas, thawed
1½ cups grated sharp Cheddar cheese
1 cup pitted ripe olives

On the day before serving, cook chicken, following recipe for chicken broth on page 17. Remove chicken and cool. Discard skin and bones, cut into bite-sized pieces, wrap, and refrigerate. Strain broth and refrigerate. Next day skim off fat and reserve. Using 6 cups of the broth, cook noodles until tender and place undrained in a 3-quart casserole. Stir in cream of mushroom soup. Melt 2 tablespoons of the chicken fat and sauté onion, green pepper, and mushrooms for 5 minutes. Add to noodles along with pimiento, seasonings, chicken, ham, and peas. Add ½ cup cheese and all but 6 of the olives and mix gently until blended. Slice remaining olives and place on top; sprinkle with remaining cheese. Bake uncovered at 325 degrees for 1 hour. (Casserole may be made in the morning and chilled. If this has been done, bake for 1¾ hours.) *Serves 10.*

POTLUCK SUPPER CASSEROLE

1 3-pound whole chicken
2 tablespoons salt
1 medium onion, peeled and quartered
½ teaspoon poultry seasoning
1 small bay leaf

1 8-ounce package seasoned bread stuffing mix
4 tablespoons butter
½ cup flour
4 cups chicken broth
6 eggs, lightly beaten

Place chicken in a saucepan. Add 5 cups water, salt, onion, poultry seasoning, and bay leaf. Cover, bring to a boil, reduce heat, and simmer for 1 hour, or until chicken is tender. Remove chicken to cool. Strain broth and reserve 4 cups liquid. Meanwhile, prepare stuffing mix following package directions for dry dressing. Spread in a buttered shallow baking dish. Remove skin from chicken; cut meat into slices wherever possible, but trim all meat from bones. Place chicken over stuffing.

In a saucepan melt 4 tablespoons butter, add flour, and stir in chicken broth. Continue to stir until thickened and smooth. Add a little of the sauce to the beaten eggs, return eggs to sauce, and stir 1 minute more. Pour sauce over chicken and bake uncovered at 325 degrees for 45 minutes, or until set. Prepare mushroom and sour cream sauce.

MUSHROOM AND SOUR CREAM SAUCE:

1 can condensed cream of mushroom soup, undiluted
¼ cup milk

½ pint sour cream
2 tablespoons minced parsley

Combine all ingredients in a small saucepan and heat over low flame. Cut casserole into squares, spoon sauce on top. *Serves 12.*

SPRING CHICKEN SOUFFLÉ

1 can condensed cream of chicken soup, undiluted
½ cup shredded Swiss cheese
½ cup grated Parmesan cheese
1 green onion, chopped
1 tablespoon minced parsley
½ teaspoon salt
¼ teaspoon dry mustard
⅛ teaspoon nutmeg
Dash pepper
6 eggs, separated
1 10-ounce package frozen chopped broccoli, thawed
1 cup diced cooked chicken

In the top of a good-sized double boiler combine soup, Swiss cheese, ¼ cup grated Parmesan cheese, onion, parsley, and seasonings. Set over simmering water and stir gently until cheese is melted. Remove from heat, and with a wooden spoon blend in egg yolks, one at a time; then add broccoli and chicken. Beat egg whites until they hold peaks, and fold gently into the chicken mixture. Generously butter a straight-sided 8-inch-by-4-inch baking dish, pour in the soufflé mixture, and sprinkle with ¼ cup grated Parmesan cheese. Bake at 375 degrees for 30 minutes, or until set. Serve immediately. *Serves 6.*

QUICK CHICKEN RAREBIT

2 large tomatoes
½ teaspoon salt
Dash paprika
1 tablespoon butter
1 12-ounce jar Welsh rarebit
1½ cups hot chicken broth
2 cups cooked chicken, diced
1 tablespoon minced parsley

Cut tomatoes into ½-inch slices and place in a buttered baking dish in a single layer. Season with salt and paprika and dot with butter. Heat Welsh rarebit in the top of a double boiler over hot water; stir in hot chicken broth and stir until smooth. Add chicken, heat briefly, then pour over tomatoes. Bake uncovered at 350 degrees for 15 minutes. Sprinkle with parsley. *Serves 4.*

DIXIE CHICKEN WITH CORNPONE

1 medium onion, chopped
1 green pepper, seeded and chopped
3 stalks celery, sliced
4 tablespoons butter
¼ cup flour
2 chicken bouillon cubes
1 teaspoon seasoned salt
1½ cups milk
1 teaspoon Worcestershire sauce
1 tablespoon prepared mustard
3 cups coarsely cut cooked chicken
1 cup black-eyed peas, canned or frozen and thawed
1 15-ounce package cornbread mix

Sauté onion, green pepper, and celery in butter until tender. Stir in flour, add bouillon cubes and seasoned salt, and blend in milk. Stir until sauce is bubbling and thickened. Season with Worcestershire sauce and mustard. Add chicken and peas, combine well, and heat briefly. Butter a shallow, wide baking dish and pour in the chicken mixture. Prepare cornbread according to package directions and spoon around perimeter of dish, leaving the center open. Bake uncovered at 400 degrees for 20 minutes. Serves 6.

EASY MAKE-AHEAD CHICKEN CASSEROLE

1 2-pound fryer, cut up
¼ cup salad oil
1 can condensed cream of mushroom soup, undiluted
½ soup can milk
¼ teaspoon poultry seasoning
1 small bay leaf
½ teaspoon salt
Dash cayenne pepper
4 carrots, quartered
6 small white onions, peeled
1 10-ounce package frozen lima beans

In a large skillet, brown chicken pieces in oil on all sides. Remove chicken and pour off remaining oil. Stir cream of mushroom soup

CASSEROLES

into the same skillet, slowly blend in milk, and add remaining ingredients. Cover and simmer for 20 minutes. Place chicken in a casserole and pour vegetables and sauce over it; cover and refrigerate until 1½ hours before serving. Bake chicken, covered, in a 375-degree oven for 1 hour, then remove cover and continue to bake for 15 minutes. *Serves 4.*

FIESTA CASSEROLE

1 5-pound chicken, cut up
3 teaspoons salt
2 cups white wine (Sauterne or Chablis)
1 8-ounce can tomato sauce
1 6-ounce can tomato puree
½ pint sour cream
2 tablespoons minced canned green chili peppers
½ cup halved pitted ripe olives
1 6½-ounce package corn chips, lightly crushed
1 cup grated Cheddar cheese

Place chicken in a large saucepan, add ½ cup water, 2 teaspoons salt, and wine and bring to a boil. Reduce heat, cover, and cook for 1½ hours. Remove chicken, cool, and discard skin and bones, leaving chicken in large pieces. Reserve broth for other uses. Blend together tomato sauce, tomato puree, sour cream, chili peppers, 1 teaspoon salt, and olives. Place half of the crushed corn chips in a baking dish, then half of the chicken, half of the sauce, and half of the cheese. Repeat layers in that order. Bake uncovered at 350 degrees for 30 minutes. *Serves 6.*

9
SKILLET ENTREES

CHICKEN HASH WITH MUSHROOM SAUCE

4 cups diced cooked chicken
4 cups diced pared potatoes
1 medium onion, chopped
1 green pepper, seeded and chopped
2 4-ounce cans chopped mushrooms, drained
2 teaspoons salt
½ teaspoon pepper
¼ teaspoon poultry seasoning
5 tablespoons butter
1 can condensed cream of mushroom soup, undiluted
½ soup can milk

Combine chicken, potatoes, onion, green pepper, mushrooms, and seasonings, mixing thoroughly. Melt butter in a large skillet with an ovenproof handle, preferably a cast-iron one; spread hash evenly and cook, covered, for 15 minutes, or until bottom is crusty and browned. Preheat broiler. Place uncovered skillet under broiler for 3 to 4 minutes, or until top is browned. Remove, carefully lift half of hash with spatula, and fold over other half. Place on a platter and keep warm. Pour soup in a saucepan, stir in milk, and heat briefly. Serve with hash. *Serves 8.*

SKILLET ENTREES

BUSY-DAY CHICKEN CACCIATORA

1 3-pound fryer, cut up
1 medium onion, thinly sliced
4 tablespoons salad oil
1 envelope dry spaghetti sauce mix
1 6-ounce can tomato paste
1 4-ounce can mushrooms, drained
Hot buttered spaghetti

Brown chicken and onion together in oil in a large skillet. Combine spaghetti sauce mix with tomato paste and 1½ cups water and pour over chicken. Cover and simmer 45 minutes, or until tender. Add mushrooms for the last 5 minutes of cooking time, then serve with buttered spaghetti. *Serves 4.*

CHICKEN CUTLETS WITH SAUCE

4 slices white bread
½ cup light cream
2 3-pound chickens
1½ teaspoons salt
¼ teaspoon white pepper
16 ounces (4 sticks) butter
2 eggs, beaten, plus 3 egg yolks, beaten separately
1 cup fine bread crumbs
½ pound fresh mushrooms, sliced
1 tablespoon flour
¼ cup chicken broth
1½ tablespoons lemon juice
Dash cayenne pepper

Soak bread slices in cream. Remove meat from uncooked chickens and grind very fine in a food chopper. Add 1 teaspoon salt and white pepper. Melt 2 tablespoons of the butter, add to the bread, and chop bread fine. Combine chicken and bread mixtures thoroughly and divide into 12 portions. Shape each portion into a cutlet, dip into the beaten whole eggs, then roll in the bread crumbs. Melt 4 tablespoons of butter in a skillet and brown the cutlets on both sides, adding more butter as necessary. Set aside and keep warm.

Melt 2 more tablespoons butter in the same skillet and sauté mushrooms for 5 minutes. Stir in flour until smooth. Gradually add the chicken broth and stir until boiling; simmer for 5 minutes and set aside. Melt remaining butter in the top of a double boiler, over water that is kept just below boiling. Add lemon juice and egg yolks, beating constantly with a wire whisk until mixture thickens. Remove from heat, add ½ teaspoon salt and cayenne pepper, then add mushrooms. Serve sauce over cutlets. *Serves 6.*

LAST-MINUTE CHICKEN CURRY

2 tablespoons butter
1 cup diced apple
¼ cup chopped onion
1 teaspoon curry powder
1 can condensed cream of chicken soup, undiluted
1 5-ounce can boned cooked chicken
2 cups hot cooked white rice
¼ cup toasted shredded coconut

Melt butter in a skillet and sauté apple and onion, seasoned with curry powder, for 7 minutes. Add cream of chicken soup, ½ cup water, and chicken. Cook until hot, stirring occasionally. Place rice in a shallow serving dish, spoon chicken in the center, and top with coconut. *Serves 4.*

CHICKEN IN SPICY ORANGE SAUCE

1 5-pound chicken, cut up
1½ teaspoons salt
½ teaspoon paprika
4 ounces (1 stick) butter
⅛ teaspoon ground cloves
⅛ teaspoon ground cinnamon
1 cup orange juice
1 avocado
1 cup mandarin oranges

Wash chicken pieces and sprinkle with salt and paprika. Melt butter in a deep skillet; brown chicken on all sides, then sprinkle with cloves and cinnamon. Add orange juice, cover, and simmer 1 hour. Cut avocado crosswise into thick slices. Place chicken on a platter and surround with avocado and mandarin orange slices. Skim fat from sauce left in skillet and drizzle over top. *Serves 6.*

SKILLET ENTREES

CHICKEN AND CHESTNUT STEW

4 ounces (1 stick) butter
2 large fryers, cut up
3 medium onions, chopped
3 teaspoons salt
1 teaspoon paprika

2 tablespoons flour
1 8-ounce can tomato sauce
1 pound uncooked chestnuts, peeled

Melt butter in a large skillet and brown several pieces of chicken at a time until all are browned on all sides. Add onions; cover and cook over medium heat for 10 minutes. Mix salt, paprika, and flour together and stir evenly into chicken, then mix tomato sauce with ½ cup water and stir slowly into the pan. Add chestnuts, cover, and cook over low heat for 1½ hours. If mixture becomes too dry, add a bit more water. *Serves 6.*

CHICKEN CACCIATORA

1 3-pound fryer, cut up
¼ cup olive oil
2 medium onions, thinly sliced
1 cup sliced mushrooms
2 cloves garlic, minced
1 1-pound can Italian-style peeled tomatoes
1 8-ounce can tomato sauce
2 tablespoons fresh parsley, chopped

½ teaspoon thyme
½ teaspoon oregano
½ teaspoon crushed bay leaf
1 teaspoon salt
¼ teaspoon pepper
½ cup dry red wine
Hot buttered spaghetti
⅓ cup grated Parmesan cheese

In a large skillet, brown chicken on both sides in olive oil; remove from pan. In the same oil sauté onions, mushrooms, and garlic for 5 minutes. Spoon off excess oil, return chicken to pan, and add next 8 ingredients, mixing gently. Cover and simmer for 45 minutes over very low heat. Add wine, turn chicken, and simmer 15 minutes longer. Arrange spaghetti on a serving platter, sprinkle with Parmesan cheese, and place chicken and sauce on top. *Serves 4.*

CARIBBEAN CREOLE

2 medium onions, chopped
½ cup salad oil
1 fryer, cut up
1½ pounds lean boneless pork, cubed
2 cloves garlic, minced
1 eggplant, diced
6 carrots, sliced
4 medium potatoes, peeled and cubed
1 tablespoon salt
1 teaspoon pepper
½ teaspoon thyme
½ teaspoon marjoram
1 tablespoon curry powder

Sauté onions in oil until golden and remove from skillet. Brown chicken in the same oil and set aside, then brown pork cubes. Return onions and chicken to pan, cover, and cook slowly for ½ hour, stirring frequently. Add remaining ingredients and 2 cups water and mix gently. Cook, covered, for an additional 45 minutes. Serves 6.

EXOTIC SPICE CHICKEN

4 chicken legs and thighs
1 teaspoon salt
½ teaspoon ground ginger
3 medium onions, thinly sliced
5½ tablespoons butter
1 15½-ounce can lima beans
¼ teaspoon ground cloves
½ teaspoon cumin powder
1½ teaspoons ground coriander
½ teaspoon ground cardamon
¼ teaspoon freshly ground pepper
¼ cup dry sherry

Wash chicken parts and pat dry. Combine salt and ginger and sprinkle over chicken. Brown chicken with onions in 4 tablespoons butter. Drain lima beans, reserving liquid, and spoon lima beans over chicken. Reduce heat and cover. Meanwhile, in a small saucepan, melt 1½ tablespoons butter, add spices, and simmer over low heat, stirring, for 1 minute. Add liquid from lima beans and sherry; simmer, stirring occasionally, for 5 minutes. Pour sauce over chicken, cover, and simmer 45 minutes more. Serves 4.

SKILLET ENTREES

CHICKEN-NOODLE CASSEROLE

2 tablespoons butter
½ cup chopped green onions
2 tablespoons minced parsley
3 cups thin noodles
3 cups fresh or canned chicken broth
½ teaspoon monosodium glutamate
2 teaspoons salt
½ teaspoon grated lemon peel
2 tablespoons dry sherry
½ pint sour cream
2 cups diced cooked chicken
¼ cup toasted slivered almonds

Melt butter in a large skillet and sauté onions and parsley until golden Add noodles, chicken broth, monosodium glutamate, and salt, stirring well to combine. Cover and cook over low heat for 30 minutes. Add lemon peel, sherry, sour cream, and chicken, blending well. Cover and cook over low heat for 5 more minutes. Turn into serving dish and top with toasted almonds. *Serves 4.*

OMELET WITH CHICKEN LIVER FILLING

FILLING:

¼ pound chicken livers, coarsely chopped
1 green onion, chopped
½ cup sliced mushrooms
1 tablespoon butter
¼ cup dry sherry

Sauté chicken livers, onion, and mushrooms in butter for 5 minutes. Add sherry, cover, and remove from heat. Keep warm. Meanwhile prepare omelet.

OMELET:

3 eggs
Dash salt
Dash pepper
1½ tablespoons butter

Beat eggs with salt and pepper only until whites and yolks are blended. Melt butter to bubbling in a skillet, pour in egg mixture, and pull back edges with a spatula, letting the uncooked mix run toward the edges until no more liquid will move. Cover half the omelet with half the filling and fold omelet in half; reduce heat to lowest temperature and cook 2 minutes more. Remove to a heated platter, place remaining filling alongside omelet, and serve immediately. *Serves 1 or 2.*

CHICKEN LIVER RISOTTO

4 ounces (1 stick) butter
½ cup finely chopped onion
1 pound chicken livers, halved
½ cup chopped fresh mushrooms
½ red pepper, chopped
1½ teaspoons salt
¼ teaspoon pepper
2 cups uncooked long-grain white rice
½ cup Marsala
4 cups boiling chicken stock
Grated Parmesan cheese

Melt butter in a large skillet or flameproof casserole. Sauté onion, chicken livers, mushrooms, and red pepper for 8 minutes. Season with salt and pepper. Add rice and stir until evenly browned. Add Marsala and boiling chicken stock, reduce heat to a simmer, cover, and cook until rice is tender and all liquid has been absorbed, adding more stock if necessary. Sprinkle generously with Parmesan cheese and serve. *Serves 8.*

MELTED CHICKEN

4 tablespoons butter
1 clove garlic, minced
1 fryer, cut up
1 medium onion, chopped
1 teaspoon salt
Dash pepper
1 8-ounce can tomato sauce
¼ teaspoon summer savory
1 cup cubed Monterey Jack cheese

Heat butter with garlic in a skillet and brown chicken and onion together; season with salt and pepper. Add tomato sauce and savory, reduce heat, and cover. Simmer for 45 minutes, or until chicken is fork-tender. Sprinkle Monterey Jack cheese over chicken, cover, and cook 5 minutes more, or until cheese is melted. *Serves 4.*

SKILLET ENTREES

SWEET AND SOUR CHICKEN

2½ pounds meaty chicken parts
6 tablespoons salad oil
2 tablespoons soy sauce
2 green peppers, thinly sliced
1½ cups diagonally sliced celery

1 medium onion, thinly sliced
1 cup crushed pineapple with liquid
¼ cup brown sugar
½ cup catsup
½ cup garlic-flavored wine vinegar

Brown chicken in 4 tablespoons salad oil. Reduce heat, cover, and cook for 10 minutes. Sprinkle with soy sauce and cook 10 minutes more; remove from pan. If pan is dry, add the 2 tablespoons salad oil. Sauté green peppers, celery, and onion for 7 to 8 minutes. Return chicken to pan, add remaining ingredients, and simmer, covered, for 35 to 40 minutes, or until chicken is quite tender. Serves 4.

PARTY CHICKEN LIVER CASSEROLE

4 tablespoons butter
1 pound mushrooms, sliced
1½ cups diagonally sliced celery
½ cup chopped onions
2 pounds chicken livers, washed

1 teaspoon salt
¼ cup flour
½ cup dry sherry
1 pint sour cream
2 tablespoons minced parsley
Hot cooked white rice

Place 2 tablespoons butter in each of two large skillets and turn heat high. Place mushrooms, celery, and onions in one pan. Sprinkle livers with salt and flour and place in second pan. Stir both pans occasionally until vegetables are golden and chicken livers are well browned on all sides. Place vegetables in a heated serving dish and keep warm, adding livers to vegetables as they are cooked. Pour sherry into the pan in which the livers were cooked and bring to a boil, scraping browned particles from pan. Reduce heat to simmer and add sour cream; stir gently but do not boil. Pour sour cream sauce over livers, sprinkle with parsley, and serve with hot rice. *Serves 6.*

CHICKEN PILAF

1 fryer, cut up
1 cup finely chopped onion
8 tablespoons butter
1½ teaspoons salt
¼ teaspoon pepper
¼ teaspoon oregano
3 tablespoons tomato paste
2 cups chicken broth
1 cup uncooked long-grain white rice

Brown chicken and onion in 4 tablespoons butter. Season with salt, pepper, and oregano, then add tomato paste and ½ cup water. Cover and simmer for 45 minutes, or until chicken is tender. Remove chicken to a baking dish and keep warm in a very slow oven. Add chicken broth to pan drippings, heat to a boil, and add rice; reduce heat, cover, and simmer for 20 minutes. Heat remaining 4 tablespoons butter until light brown and pour over rice. Top with chicken, cover, and heat for 5 minutes. *Serves 4.*

SKILLET LEMON CHICKEN

1 teaspoon garlic puree
1 teaspoon salt
1 medium onion, sliced into rings
1 tablespoon paprika
½ teaspoon thyme
½ teaspoon oregano
½ cup lemon juice
¼ cup salad oil
1 3-pound fryer, cut up

Make a marinade by combining all ingredients but chicken in order given. Place chicken in a shallow pan, pour marinade over it, and refrigerate all day or overnight if possible, turning and basting several times. One hour before serving, heat an electric skillet to 360 degrees. Brown chicken on all sides in the sauce for about 15 minutes; reduce temperature to 215 degrees, cover, and simmer for 45 minutes, basting frequently with sauce. Remove from sauce and serve. *Serves 4.*

SKILLET ENTREES

OUTRIGGER SPECIAL

1 large green pepper, cut into 1-inch strips
1 clove garlic, minced
2 tablespoons salad oil
2 cans condensed cream of chicken soup, undiluted
1 13-ounce can pineapple tidbits with liquid
2 cups cubed cooked chicken
2 tablespoons soy sauce
3 cups hot cooked white rice
¼ cup toasted slivered almonds

In a large skillet sauté green pepper strips and garlic in oil until tender. Stir in cream of chicken soup and pineapple liquid, blending well. Add the pineapple tidbits and cubed chicken and season with soy sauce; heat over a low flame for 6 to 8 minutes. Spoon over hot, fluffy rice, then sprinkle with toasted almonds. *Serves 6.*

SMOTHERED CHICKEN

4 tablespoons butter
1 3-pound fryer, cut up and skinned
1 teaspoon salt
¼ teaspoon pepper
1½ teaspoons crushed dill weed
2 cups sliced fresh mushrooms
¼ cup chopped green onion
2 tablespoons flour
½ cup white wine
1 cup sour cream
½ teaspoon grated lemon rind

Melt butter in a large skillet. Sauté chicken gently on all sides, season with salt and pepper, and remove from pan. To pan drippings add dill weed, mushrooms, and green onion. Cook over low heat for 3 minutes, then stir in flour and white wine until smooth. Add sour cream and blend. Return chicken to pan, cover, and cook over low heat for 40 minutes, or until chicken is tender, stirring occasionally. Sprinkle with lemon rind just before serving. *Serves 4.*

10
CHICKEN BREASTS

CURRIED CHICKEN AND VEGETABLE SKILLET

4 whole chicken breasts
3 tablespoons butter
½ cup diagonally sliced celery
½ cup sliced onion rings
2 teaspoons curry powder
1 teaspoon garlic puree
1 can condensed cream of chicken soup, undiluted

1 15-ounce can asparagus spears, cut up
1 6-ounce can water chestnuts, sliced
1 tablespoon cornstarch
Hot steamed white rice

Brown chicken on all sides in butter in a roomy skillet. Add celery, onion rings, curry powder, and garlic puree and simmer until vegetables look transparent. Stir in cream of chicken soup, cover, and simmer for 40 minutes. Add well-drained cut asparagus and water chestnuts, and heat for 5 minutes. Combine 2 tablespoons water and cornstarch and stir into skillet to thicken sauce. Remove and serve with hot steamed rice. *Serves 4.*

CHICKEN BREASTS

BRAISED CHICKEN BREASTS

3 whole chicken breasts, halved
4 tablespoons butter
1 teaspoon salt
¼ teaspoon pepper
1 medium onion, chopped
½ pound small fresh button mushrooms
3 tablespoons flour
½ cup chicken broth
1 cup Sauterne
½ cup light cream

Brown chicken on both sides in butter and sprinkle with salt and pepper; remove from pan. In the remaining drippings, sauté onions and mushrooms for 8 minutes. Stir in flour, then add chicken broth, Sauterne, and cream, stirring to loosen any particles. Add chicken, reduce heat, cover, and simmer for 45 minutes. Serves 6.

CHICKEN AND FRUIT MEDLEY

6 whole chicken breasts, halved
½ cup flour
½ teaspoon ground ginger
1 teaspoon curry powder
1 teaspoon salt
4 tablespoons butter
1 9-ounce can pineapple chunks
1 11-ounce can mandarin oranges
1 tablespoon lemon juice
1 tart apple, cored and cubed

Remove skin and bones from chicken breasts. In a clean paper bag, combine flour, ginger, curry powder and salt. Add chicken and shake until well coated; reserve flour mixture. In a large skillet melt butter and brown chicken on both sides. Remove to a baking dish.

   Add leftover flour mixture to remaining drippings in pan; stir over low heat until smooth. Slowly add liquid from pineapple chunks and mandarin oranges, then the lemon juice, stirring constantly. Simmer until thickened. Meanwhile, spread pineapple chunks, mandarin oranges, and apple over chicken, then add sauce. Cover and bake at 350 degrees for 1 hour. Serves 6.

CHICKEN BREASTS GALA

½ cup flour
1 teaspoon garlic salt
½ teaspoon paprika
6 whole chicken breasts, halved
6 tablespoons salad oil
1 4-ounce can button mushrooms

1 can condensed cream of mushroom soup, undiluted
½ cup chicken broth
½ cup orange juice
½ cup Chablis
¼ teaspoon nutmeg
1 tablespoon brown sugar
2 cups diagonally sliced carrots

In a clean paper bag combine flour, garlic salt, and paprika. Add chicken pieces and shake until well coated. Heat oil in a large skillet and brown chicken breasts on both sides. Drain mushrooms, reserving liquid, and add mushrooms to chicken. Blend together mushroom liquid, cream of mushroom soup, chicken broth, orange juice, and Chablis; add nutmeg and brown sugar and stir until smooth. Pour this mixture over chicken and simmer, covered, for 15 minutes. Add carrots, cover, and simmer 20 minutes more. Serves 6.

CHICKEN BROCCOLI CASSEROLE

3 whole chicken breasts
1 13¾-ounce can chicken broth
2 10-ounce packages frozen broccoli spears
2 cans condensed cream of chicken soup, undiluted

1 cup mayonnaise
1 teaspoon lemon juice
Dash nutmeg
½ cup shredded sharp Cheddar cheese
½ cup toasted bread crumbs

Cook chicken breasts with chicken broth in a covered saucepan for ½ hour. Remove and cool; remove skin and bones, leaving pieces whole if possible. Cut into slices and set aside. Cook broccoli spears in remaining broth until barely tender. Drain and

CHICKEN BREASTS

place in a shallow, buttered baking dish. Place chicken slices on top. In a bowl combine cream of chicken soup, mayonnaise, lemon juice, and nutmeg. Blend well. Pour over chicken and sprinkle with Cheddar cheese, then with toasted bread crumbs. Bake uncovered at 350 degrees for ½ hour. *Serves 6.*

CHICKEN JUBILEE

3 whole chicken breasts, halved
½ cup Dixie Fry
¼ teaspoon garlic salt
4 tablespoons butter
1 1-pound can pitted dark cherries, drained
1 cup Sauterne

Shake chicken in a paper bag containing Dixie Fry and garlic salt. Melt butter in a skillet or chafing dish and brown chicken on all sides. Add cherries and Sauterne, cover, and simmer for 35 minutes, or until chicken is fork-tender. *Serves 6.*

CHICKEN KIEV

4 whole chicken breasts
2 teaspoons salt
4 tablespoons minced parsley
4 tablespoons green onion
4 ounces (1 stick) chilled butter
1 cup shredded sharp Cheddar cheese
½ cup flour
2 eggs, slightly beaten
¾ cup fine bread crumbs
Oil for frying

Carefully remove skin and bones from chicken breasts and cut in half lengthwise. Place each piece between 2 sheets of plastic film and pound with mallet until chicken is about ¼ inch thick. Remove film. Sprinkle each piece with salt, parsley, and green onion. Cut butter into 8 slices, cut each slice in half, and place 2 halves along one end of each piece of chicken. Sprinkle chicken with Cheddar cheese and, starting at the buttered end, roll each piece tightly, tucking in the ends to seal, jellyroll fashion. Sprinkle rolls with flour and dip in beaten eggs, then roll in bread crumbs. Place on a baking sheet and chill for at least 1 hour before cooking. About 1 hour before serving time, heat oil in deep-fryer to 375 degrees, drop in chicken rolls, and fry about 5 minutes, or until golden-crisp. Remove to baking sheet and bake uncovered in a 325-degree oven for 30 minutes. *Serves 4.*

SOPHISTICATED CHICKEN SAUTÉ

2 whole chicken breasts, halved
1 lemon, cut into wedges
1 teaspoon salt
¼ teaspoon pepper
4 tablespoons butter

2 tablespoons sliced green onion
¼ teaspoon dried thyme
1 cup Rhine wine
8 moist dried apricot halves
⅓ cup toasted slivered almonds

Wash chicken and pat dry; rub skins generously with lemon, squeezing out juice. Sprinkle on salt and pepper. Heat butter in a skillet and brown chicken quickly on both sides. Sprinkle on onion, reduce heat, and add thyme and half of the wine. Place 2 apricot halves on each piece of chicken, cover skillet tightly, and simmer for 10 minutes. Turn chicken and replace same apricots on top; simmer 15 minutes more. Remove chicken with apricots onto a heated platter and keep warm. Add remaining wine to drippings, cook over high heat, and stir, loosening stuck particles, until liquid is slightly reduced. Add almonds and heat 1 minute more. Pour sauce over chicken and serve. *Serves 4.*

CHICKEN PAGO PAGO

3 whole chicken breasts
6 tablespoons butter
1 6-ounce can frozen pine-apple-orange concentrate
1 teaspoon ginger
1 teaspoon soy sauce

6 cups crisp Chinese noodles
1 avocado, peeled and sliced
1 tablespoon lemon juice
1 11-ounce can mandarin oranges, drained
½ cup shredded coconut

CHICKEN BREASTS

Remove skin and bones from chicken breasts. Cut in half lengthwise and flatten each piece with a blow from the side of a cleaver. Melt butter in a skillet and lightly brown chicken on both sides, a few pieces at a time. Remove to a shallow baking pan. When all pieces are done, add undiluted fruit concentrate, ginger, and soy sauce to drippings in pan; stir until dissolved and warm. Brush some of this sauce on the chicken, place in a 350-degree oven, and bake uncovered for 30 to 35 minutes, basting often with sauce. Place 1 cup Chinese noodles on each of 6 plates. Sprinkle avocado slices with lemon juice and arrange some avocado and mandarin orange on each mound of noodles, then cover with a piece of chicken. Pour some fruit sauce over each piece of chicken, and top with shredded coconut. *Serves 6.*

SKILLET PARTY CHICKEN

1 cup sour cream
2 tablespoons fresh chopped parsley
½ teaspoon garlic salt
1 tablespoon fresh lemon juice
3 whole chicken breasts
4 tablespoons butter
2 4-ounce cans button mushrooms
2 medium onions, thinly sliced
2 8-ounce packages frozen artichoke hearts, thawed
½ teaspoon thyme
½ teaspoon basil
1 teaspoon salt
¼ teaspoon pepper
1 chicken bouillon cube
Hot cooked white rice

Early in the day, combine first 4 ingredients in a bowl. Cover and refrigerate until serving time. To prepare chicken, remove skin and bones from chicken breasts and cut into bite-sized pieces. Set electric skillet for low heat, melt butter, and brown chicken pieces slowly on all sides. Drain mushrooms, reserving liquid. Add onions, mushrooms, artichoke hearts, and seasonings to chicken and mix gently. Heat mushroom liquid with bouillon cube; pour over chicken and simmer for 5 to 10 minutes, or until tender. Serve chicken over hot rice and top with cold parsley–sour cream sauce. *Serves 4.*

ROSY BAKED CHICKEN

2 whole chicken breasts, halved
½ cup Dixie Fry
6 tablespoons butter
3 large, firm tomatoes
½ teaspoon tarragon
1 tablespoon flour
1 cup light cream

Shake chicken breasts in a bag with Dixie Fry until well coated. Melt butter in a skillet over medium-high heat and brown chicken well on all sides. Remove chicken to a baking dish. Cut 4 thick slices from tomatoes and dip in the same Dixie Fry. Brown tomatoes on both sides in drippings used for chicken, and remove to the baking dish. Chop remainder of tomatoes very fine and add to drippings, sprinkle with tarragon, and simmer over low heat for 3 minutes. Stir in flour, then slowly add cream, stirring until smooth and thick. Pour sauce over chicken and tomatoes and bake covered at 350 degrees for 1 hour. *Serves 4.*

FISHERMAN'S WHARF CHICKEN

1 pint sour cream
1 tablespoon lemon juice
1 tablespoon minced parsley
1 teaspoon tarragon
1 teaspoon salt
½ teaspoon thyme
¼ teaspoon garlic powder
¼ teaspoon paprika
3 whole chicken breasts, halved
1 cup packaged cornflake crumbs
4 tablespoons butter
½ pound tiny shrimp, cooked
1 avocado, cubed

Combine sour cream with lemon juice and seasonings. Dip chicken breasts into this mixture, then roll in cornflake crumbs. Reserve remaining sour cream mixture. Melt butter in a shallow baking dish and place chicken in butter, skin side down. Bake uncovered at 350 degrees for 45 minutes, then turn and bake 15 minutes more. Just before chicken is done, add shrimp and avocado to remaining sour cream. Heat very gently and serve over chicken. *Serves 6.*

CHICKEN BREASTS

DOUBLE-GOOD HAM AND CHICKEN

4 whole chicken breasts
¼ cup flour
2 teaspoons salt
1 teaspoon paprika
4 tablespoons butter
4 slices cooked ham,
  ¼ inch thick

1 teaspoon dried savory
2 tablespoons chopped
  celery leaves
8 mushrooms, sliced
½ cup Sauterne
½ pint sour cream

Wash chicken breasts and pat dry. Combine flour, salt, and paprika in a paper bag; add chicken and shake until well coated. Reserve seasoned flour. Melt butter in a skillet and brown chicken delicately on all sides. Meanwhile, place ham slices in a buttered baking dish and sprinkle with savory and celery leaves. When chicken is browned, place on ham slices. Toss mushroom slices in pan drippings, add Sauterne, and stir to loosen stuck particles. Add remaining seasoned flour to sour cream to prevent curdling while baking, then stir sour cream into Sauterne mixture, blend, and pour over chicken. Cover and bake at 350 degrees for 1 hour. Serves 4.

EASY CHICKEN PÉRIGOURDINE

8 whole chicken breasts,
  bones removed
4 tablespoons butter, more
  if needed
12 large fresh mushrooms
⅓ cup flour
¼ teaspoon salt
1 13¾-ounce can chicken
  broth

2 tablespoons light cream
1 cup canned Hollandaise
  sauce
Dash cayenne pepper
1 tablespoon lemon juice
¼ cup dry sherry

In a large, heavy, ovenproof skillet, sauté chicken breasts in butter on both sides, adding more butter if necessary, until golden; remove. Slice 8 mushrooms and sauté in the drippings for 5 minutes, then remove. Stir flour into drippings; mince 4 mushrooms and add to drippings with salt. Slowly stir in chicken broth and cream; continue to stir until sauce is thick and smooth.

Place chicken breasts in sauce; cover and simmer for about 25 minutes, or until chicken is tender. Meanwhile, place Hollandaise sauce in a small bowl and beat with rotary beater until smooth, adding cayenne pepper and lemon juice. Refrigerate. When chicken is done, stir in mushroom slices and sherry. Spread Hollandaise sauce over chicken and place under broiler for 1 minute, or until barely golden. Serve immediately in skillet. *Serves 8.*

CHICKEN-RICE CASSEROLE WITH CHEESE SAUCE

1 cup uncooked long-grain white rice
1 4-ounce can mushroom pieces, drained
2 tablespoons butter
3 whole chicken breasts, boned and halved
¼ cup salad oil
1 can condensed onion soup, undiluted

In a large skillet, sauté rice and mushroom pieces in butter until well browned; remove to an 11 x 7 x 1½-inch baking dish. Brown chicken breasts in oil until golden; place in a row down the center of the baking dish. Combine onion soup and 1 cup water and pour over chicken and rice. Cover with aluminum foil and bake at 350 degrees for 50 minutes, or until all liquid has been absorbed and chicken is tender. Serve with cheese sauce.

CHEESE SAUCE:

2 tablespoons butter
2 tablespoons flour
½ teaspoon salt
Dash nutmeg
1¼ cups milk
1 cup shredded American cheese

Melt butter in a small saucepan over low heat. Stir in flour, seasonings, and milk. Simmer, stirring all the while, until sauce thickens and bubbles. Add American cheese and stir until melted. *Serves 6.*

11

CREAMED CHICKEN

CREAMED CHICKEN LIVERS ON TOAST

6 slices bacon
4 tablespoons butter
1 pound chicken livers, quartered
1 pound fresh mushrooms, sliced
¼ cup chopped green onion
1 teaspoon garlic salt
¼ teaspoon freshly ground pepper
2 tablespoons flour
¾ cup chicken broth
¾ cup cooking sherry
1 tablespoon wine vinegar
6 slices toast, quartered diagonally

Fry bacon until crisp, drain and crumble, and set aside. Pour off all but 1 tablespoon of the drippings, melt butter in pan, and sauté chicken livers, mushrooms, and green onion, seasoning with garlic salt and pepper, for 8 minutes. Remove with slotted spoon. Stir flour into drippings and blend in chicken broth, sherry, and vinegar; bring to a boil, stirring until smooth and thickened. Reduce heat, return chicken liver mixture and bacon bits to pan, and reheat. Serve on toast points. *Serves 6.*

CREAMED CHICKEN

BUFFET SUPPER
CHAFING DISH CHICKEN*

3 tablespoons butter
½ cup finely minced green onions
¼ cup flour
1 13¾-ounce can or 1½ cups chicken broth
1½ cups light cream
2 teaspoons salt
1 teaspoon monosodium glutamate
Dash cayenne
Dash nutmeg
2 egg yolks, lightly beaten
3 cups diced cooked chicken
1½ cups canned sliced mushrooms, drained
Hot cooked white rice

Melt butter and sauté onions over low heat for 8 minutes. Stir in flour, slowly blend in chicken broth and cream, and add seasonings. Continue to stir until sauce is smooth and thick. Add a little of the sauce to the egg yolks, then return eggs to sauce; continue to simmer and stir for 1 more minute. Add chicken and mushrooms and gently heat. Serve with mounds of fluffy cooked rice. Serves 8.

CHICKEN AVOCADO NEWBURG

4 tablespoons butter
4 tablespoons flour
1 egg yolk, beaten
1½ cans canned or fresh chicken broth
1 teaspoon salt
Dash pepper
Dash nutmeg
1 tablespoon lemon juice
3 tablespoons dry sherry
2 cups diced cooked chicken
1 avocado, peeled and quartered
4 patty shells or 16 toast triangles

Melt butter in a saucepan and stir in flour. Add beaten egg yolk to cold chicken broth and gradually add to butter mixture, stirring continuously. Add seasonings, lemon juice, and sherry, and con-

* This may be prepared in a chafing dish, or it may be prepared in a skillet and placed in the chafing dish later to be reheated.

tinue to stir until mixture thickens and comes to a gentle boil. Fold in chicken, cover, and heat over low flame for 5 minutes. Slice avocado quarters, add to mixture, and heat briefly; serve in patty shells or over toast triangles. *Serves 4.*

CREAMED CHICKEN WITH ASPARAGUS

3 tablespoons butter
2 tablespoons flour
1 3-ounce package cream cheese
1 teaspoon salt
Dash paprika
1 cup milk

1 cup chicken broth
2 cups diced cooked chicken
2 cups cooked or canned cut asparagus, drained
1 tablespoon chopped pimiento
16 toast tips

Melt butter and stir in flour and cream cheese until smooth; add salt and paprika. Slowly blend in milk, then chicken broth, stirring constantly until boiling and slightly thickened. Add chicken, asparagus, and pimiento and heat over low flame to boiling. Serve on toast tips. *Serves 4.*

CHICKEN-CRAB BOATS

3 medium acorn squash
1 teaspoon salt
4 tablespoons butter
1 pint sour cream
1 tablespoon tarragon vinegar
1½ cups diced cooked or canned chicken

1 cup fresh or canned crab meat
½ cup grated Parmesan cheese
Dash paprika

Wash and cut squash in half lengthwise. Scoop out center, removing seeds and fibers. Place, cut side down, on a lightly buttered baking sheet and bake at 350 degrees for 40 minutes. Turn cut

CREAMED CHICKEN

side up, sprinkle with salt, and dot with butter; continue baking for 15 to 20 minutes, or until tender. Just before squash is done, place sour cream in a saucepan, stir in vinegar, add chicken and crab meat, and heat gently, without allowing mixture to boil. Remove squash to serving dish, fill centers with creamy mixture, sprinkle with Parmesan cheese and paprika, and serve. *Serves 6.*

SWISS CHICKEN CRÊPES

CHICKEN FILLING AND SAUCE:

- 5 tablespoons butter
- 5 tablespoons flour
- ½ teaspoon salt
- Dash white pepper
- 1 cup light cream
- 1 cup chicken broth
- ½ teaspoon Worcestershire sauce
- 2 tablespoons chopped parsley
- 1 cup grated Swiss cheese
- ¾ cup Sauterne
- 2 cups finely diced cooked chicken
- Dash paprika

Melt butter and stir in flour, salt, and pepper. Blend in cream, chicken broth, and Worcestershire sauce; continue to stir until smooth and thick. Add parsley, Swiss cheese, and Sauterne and stir until cheese is melted. Place 1 cup of sauce in a bowl; add chicken and paprika. Place remaining sauce in the top of a double boiler and keep warm over hot water. Meanwhile, make crêpes.

CRÊPES:

- 1 cup flour
- ¼ teaspoon salt
- 1½ cups milk
- 3 eggs
- 2 tablespoons butter
- 1 avocado, peeled and sliced
- Grated Swiss cheese

Combine first 4 ingredients in order listed and beat with a rotary beater until smooth. Using 1 teaspoon butter per crêpe, melt butter in a 7-inch skillet, pour in 2 to 3 tablespoons of batter, and tip pan until batter is very thin. When crêpe is dry on top and nicely browned on the bottom, remove from skillet and place a heaping spoonful of chicken mixture across the center. Roll up and place in a shallow baking dish. Repeat until 6 crêpes are done. Arrange avocado slices on top, pour on warm cream sauce, and sprinkle with grated Swiss cheese. Bake uncovered at 375 degrees for 15 minutes, then place under broiler for 1 minute. *Serves 6.*

CHICKEN À LA KING

4 ounces (1 stick) butter
½ cup flour
Dash paprika
¼ cup scalded milk
½ cup heavy cream
2 cups hot chicken broth
2 egg yolks, well beaten

2 cups cooked chicken, cut into strips
1 cup sautéed sliced mushrooms
2 tablespoons sliced pimiento
1 teaspoon salt
4 to 6 patty shells

Melt butter and stir in flour and paprika. Blend in milk, cream, and chicken broth and bring to a boil, stirring constantly. Blend a little of the sauce into the egg yolks, then return to rest of sauce. Stir in chicken, mushrooms, pimiento, and salt; adjust seasoning if necessary. Serve in patty shells. *Serves 4 to 6.*

CHICKEN-FILLED PANCAKES

CREAMED CHICKEN FILLING:

3 tablespoons butter
¼ cup flour
1 teaspoon salt
¼ teaspoon poultry seasoning

Dash paprika
1½ cups milk
2 cups minced chicken

Melt butter, remove from heat, and stir in flour, seasonings, and milk. Heat, stirring constantly, until sauce is smooth and thick. Add chicken and keep warm while preparing pancakes.

PANCAKES:

1⅔ cups milk
1 egg
2 cups Bisquick

Butter for frying
8 tablespoons grated Cheddar cheese

CREAMED CHICKEN

Add milk and egg to biscuit mix all at once; beat with rotary beater until smooth. On a buttered grill pour ½ cup batter per pancake and fry until golden on both sides. Make 8 pancakes. Place ¼ cup chicken filling on half of each pancake, fold over, and place on a lightly buttered baking sheet. Top each pancake with 1 tablespoon grated Cheddar cheese and place under broiler until cheese is melted and bubbling. *Serves 4.*

ELEGANT CREAMED CHICKEN

3 *whole chicken breasts*
1½ *teaspoons salt*
½ *teaspoon poultry seasoning*
1 *10-ounce package frozen peas with onions*
1 *pound fresh mushrooms*
5 *tablespoons butter*
3 *tablespoons flour*
1 *tablespoon minced onion*
½ *teaspoon celery salt*
½ *teaspoon paprika*
½ *teaspoon oregano*
1 *teaspoon Worcestershire sauce*
½ *cup Sauterne*
1 *cup light cream*
Hot cooked white rice

Place chicken, 1 teaspoon salt, and poultry seasoning in saucepan and add water to cover. Cover saucepan and simmer for about ½ hour or until tender. Remove from broth, reserving 1 cup liquid. Remove skin and bones from meat, being careful to leave chicken in large pieces; set chicken aside.

Meanwhile, cook frozen peas with onions according to package directions. Drain and set aside. Cut stems from mushrooms, wash, and dry. Melt 2 tablespoons butter in a skillet and gently sauté mushroom caps until golden. Remove. In the same pan, melt 3 tablespoons butter and stir in flour, minced onion, ½ teaspoon salt, and the other seasonings, then slowly add reserved chicken broth and Sauterne. Stir over low heat until thickened. Cool slightly and add cream, mushrooms, peas with onions, and chicken. Reheat gently, but do not boil. Serve over hot, fluffy rice. *Serves 6.*

CHICKEN ROLL
WITH MORNAY SAUCE

5 tablespoons butter
3 tablespoons flour
1 cup half and half
1 cup chicken broth
½ teaspoon salt
⅛ teaspoon paprika
2 cups minced chicken
1 teaspoon onion juice
1 tablespoon minced parsley

⅛ teaspoon nutmeg
2 cups Bisquick
⅔ cup milk
2 tablespoons grated
 Parmesan cheese
2 tablespoons grated
 Swiss cheese
Few grains cayenne pepper

Melt 3 tablespoons butter, stir in flour, and slowly blend in half and half and chicken broth. Season with salt and paprika and cook over moderate heat, stirring constantly, until smooth and thickened. Set aside. Season chicken with onion juice, parsley, and nutmeg. Add ½ cup of the cream sauce and blend. Stir milk into Bisquick according to package directions and roll out on a floured board into a 9- by 12-inch rectangle. Spread chicken mixture not quite to the edges and roll, jellyroll fashion. Place on a buttered baking sheet and bake at 400 degrees for 35 minutes or until delicately browned. Just before biscuit mix is done, reheat remaining cream sauce, then stir in 2 tablespoons butter, cheeses, and cayenne pepper. When well blended and smooth, serve with slices of chicken roll. *Serves 4 to 6.*

12

AROUND THE WORLD

CHICKEN AND NOODLES ALLA ROMANA

1½ teaspoons salt
¼ teaspoon pepper
1 3-pound fryer, cut up
4 tablespoons olive oil
1 pound small button mushrooms
4 tablespoons minced onion
1 6-ounce can tomato paste
½ cup chopped parsley
8 ounces very thin egg noodles, cooked
1 tablespoon butter

Rub salt and pepper into chicken pieces. Heat oil in a large skillet and brown chicken on all sides; remove from pan. Sauté mushrooms and onion in drippings until soft, then return chicken to pan and add tomato paste, ¼ cup water, and parsley. Mix gently and cover pan tightly; simmer for 45 minutes. If sauce looks very thin, remove cover and let some of the liquid evaporate. Meanwhile, prepare noodles according to package directions, drain, and stir in butter. Place noodles on a platter, put chicken pieces on top, and cover with sauce. Serves 4.

AFRICAN BAKED CHICKEN

11 tablespoons butter
2 fryers, cut up
1 medium onion, chopped
1 clove garlic, minced
1 tablespoon flour
¾ cup white wine
2 teaspoons salt
½ teaspoon pepper
1 bay leaf
3 tomatoes, chopped
3 medium sweet potatoes, peeled and cubed
5 firm bananas, sliced into 1-inch pieces

Melt 8 tablespoons butter in a large skillet and sauté chicken pieces, onion, and garlic until browned, stirring often. Sprinkle with flour, then add wine, 1 cup water, salt, pepper, bay leaf, and tomatoes; stir until well mixed. Cover and cook over low heat for 20 minutes; add sweet potatoes and continue to cook for 40 minutes.

Sauté banana slices very gently in 3 tablespoons butter. Place chicken in center of platter and surround with sweet potatoes and bananas. Skim fat from gravy and serve separately. *Serves 6.*

ARROZ CON POLLO

2 strips bacon, diced
½ pound chorizos (Spanish sausages)
¼ cup olive oil
1 3- to 3½-pound fryer, cut up
1 medium onion, finely chopped
1 cup sliced fresh mushrooms
1 clove garlic, minced
1½ cups uncooked long-grain white rice
1 large tomato, peeled and chopped
1 2-ounce can pimientos, sliced
1 4-ounce can green chili peppers, sliced
6 green pitted olives, halved
1 bay leaf, crumbled
½ teaspoon oregano
Pinch Spanish saffron
2 cups chicken broth
1 cup dry white wine
Salt
Pepper
1 cup cooked peas (optional)

Fry bacon and chorizos together until bacon is crisp; remove both to a large baking dish with a slotted spoon. Add olive oil to drippings, brown chicken on all sides, and place in baking dish. In the same drippings sauté onion, mushrooms, and garlic for 5 minutes, and remove with slotted spoon to baking dish. Brown rice in remaining oil and add to casserole. In the order listed, place next 9 ingredients and salt and pepper to taste in the casserole. Cover tightly and bake at 375 degrees for 1 hour. Check to see if mixture has become dry, and add a little more chicken broth if necessary; 1 cup cooked peas may be added for last 10 minutes. *Serves 6.*

INDIVIDUAL CHICKEN AND PALM SOUFFLÉS

3 whole chicken breasts
Garlic salt
Pepper
4 tablespoons butter
¼ pound fresh mushrooms, sliced
2 teaspoons lemon juice
1 14-ounce can hearts of palm
1 tablespoon minced parsley
4 eggs, separated, plus 2 egg yolks
½ cup grated Parmesan cheese
¼ teaspoon nutmeg
¼ teaspoon salt
½ cup heavy cream

Season chicken breasts with garlic salt and pepper to taste. Melt butter in a skillet and brown chicken on both sides; cover and simmer for 20 minutes. Remove chicken from pan and let it cool slightly, then remove skin and bones and cut meat into thin strips. Add sliced mushrooms to drippings in pan, sprinkle with lemon juice, and simmer for 5 minutes. Meanwhile, drain hearts of palm and cut into ½-inch rounds. Add to mushrooms, sprinkle with parsley, and add chicken strips.

Generously butter 6 individual 4-inch ramekins and divide chicken mixture among them. Beat the 6 egg yolks until thick and pale yellow. Add Parmesan cheese, nutmeg, and salt. Whip cream until stiff and fold in gently. Beat egg whites until stiff and fold in. Divide mixture evenly, spoon over chicken, and bake at 425 degrees for 15 minutes, or until set. Serve immediately. *Serves 6.*

AUSTRIAN CHICKEN

- 2 3½-pound fryers, disjointed
- 2 teaspoons salt
- 1 teaspoon pepper
- 4 ounces (1 stick) butter
- 6 medium onions, peeled and thinly sliced
- 1½ tablespoons paprika
- ½ pint sour cream
- Packaged dumpling mix

Wash and dry chicken pieces and rub in salt and pepper on both sides. Melt butter in a skillet and sauté sliced onions and paprika for 3 minutes, stirring constantly. Add chicken pieces and brown over high heat until golden. Add ½ cup water, cover pan, and simmer chicken for 30 minutes, stirring occasionally. Gently stir in sour cream and simmer 15 minutes more. This dish is traditionally served with dumplings, which can be made with prepared dumpling mix, over which some of the sauce has been poured. *Serves 6.*

HAITIAN ONE-COURSE CHICKEN SOUP

- 1 tablespoon salt
- ½ teaspoon black pepper
- 2 fryers, cut up
- 6 tablespoons butter
- ½ pound boiled ham, cubed
- ½ teaspoon ground chili peppers
- 2 medium onions, chopped
- 3 stalks celery, sliced
- 3 medium potatoes, peeled and cubed
- 2 medium sweet potatoes, peeled and cubed
- 3 medium carrots
- 2 tablespoons flour
- 2 tablespoons tomato sauce

Rub salt and pepper into washed chicken parts. Sauté chicken in butter until browned on all sides. Add ham, 3 quarts water, chili peppers, onions, and celery. When boiling, skim the top, cover, and cook slowly for 1 hour.

Add both kinds of potatoes and carrots; continue cooking 1 more hour. Stir flour into tomato sauce, slowly add 1 cup broth, and return mixture to soup. Stir well and cook 10 minutes more. *Serves 6.*

CENTRAL AMERICAN CHICKEN WITH SWISS CHARD

1 3½-pound fryer, cut up
1 medium onion, chopped
1 bay leaf, crumbled
2 teaspoons salt, more if needed
½ teaspoon freshly ground coarse pepper, more if needed
2 pounds Swiss chard
2 tablespoons flour

Place chicken, onion, bay leaf, 2 teaspoons salt, and ½ teaspoon pepper in a large saucepan. Add 4 cups water and bring to a boil. Reduce heat, cover tightly, and simmer for 45 minutes. Clean chard and tear leaves into quarters; add to chicken and cook 20 minutes more. Add more salt and pepper if necessary. Remove chicken and chard to a warm platter and thicken remaining broth with a paste made with flour and 2 tablespoons water. Pour over chicken. *Serves 4.*

CHICKEN TACOS

3 tablespoons salad oil plus ¾ cup of same oil
6 tomatoes, peeled and chopped
1 medium onion, chopped
2 green peppers, chopped
1 teaspoon salt
½ teaspoon pepper
Dash cumin powder
1 cup chopped cooked chicken
1 tablespoon chopped seedless raisins
3 tablespoons chopped green olives
12 corn tortillas
2 eggs, beaten
Shredded lettuce (optional)
Avocado slices (optional)

Heat 3 tablespoons oil in a saucepan. Add tomatoes, onion, green peppers, salt, pepper, and cumin powder; simmer for 20 minutes, stirring occasionally. Combine chicken, raisins, and olives and mix well. Dip each tortilla in the beaten eggs and place on waxed paper. Place 1 tablespoon of the chicken mixture on each tortilla, roll it up, and fasten with a toothpick. Heat the ¾ cup oil to 375 degrees, fry tortillas for 3 minutes, drain on absorbent towels. Place on a heated serving dish and pour tomato sauce over top. If desired, garnish with shredded lettuce and avocado slices. *Serves 6.*

CHINESE WALNUT CHICKEN

3 whole chicken breasts
1 teaspoon salt
1 teaspoon sugar
3 tablespoons dry sherry
1 tablespoon soy sauce
3 tablespoons cornstarch
1 egg, beaten
¾ cup salad oil
1 cup blanched walnuts
2 teaspoons minced fresh gingerroot or 1 teaspoon powdered ginger
2 cloves garlic, minced
1 teaspoon monosodium glutamate
1 cup thinly sliced canned bamboo shoots
Hot cooked white rice or crisp Chinese noodles

Remove chicken breasts from bone, skin them, and cut into 1-inch cubes. Place cubes in a bowl together with the salt, sugar, sherry, and soy sauce. Toss well and marinate for 30 minutes. Drain, reserving the liquid. Dip chicken cubes first in cornstarch, then in egg. Heat oil in a skillet; sauté walnuts until brown and remove from pan. In the same oil, brown the chicken with the gingerroot and garlic, then add ¾ cup boiling water, monosodium glutamate, bamboo shoots, and marinade. Cover and cook slowly for 20 minutes, stirring occasionally. Add walnuts and cook for 1 minute more. Serve with hot fluffy rice or Chinese noodles. *Serves 6.*

COCONUT CHICKEN IN SPINACH

1 cup shredded coconut
1 cup milk
1 fryer, boned and cubed
2 tablespoons salad oil
2½ teaspoons salt
3 tablespoons butter
1 10-ounce package frozen spinach

Combine coconut and milk in a saucepan. Bring quickly to a boil, remove from heat, and let stand for ½ hour. Press all the liquid from the coconut into a bowl and discard the pulp. Brown chicken cubes in oil, then add 2 teaspoons salt and ½ cup water. Cover and simmer for 20 minutes. Melt butter in a small saucepan, add frozen spinach and ½ teaspoon salt, and simmer over low heat until defrosted. Drain well. Return to saucepan and combine with coconut milk, then add drained chicken; simmer for 10 minutes. Serves 6.

CHICKEN CHOW MEIN*

2 whole chicken breasts
¼ cup salad oil
1 cup diagonally sliced celery
2 medium onions, thinly sliced
1 green pepper, thinly sliced
1 cup thinly sliced mushrooms
1 1-pound can bean sprouts, drained
1 4-ounce can sliced bamboo shoots, drained
1 4-ounce can sliced water chestnuts, drained
1 7-ounce package frozen Chinese snow pea pods (sugar peas), thawed
2 cups chicken broth
2 tablespoons soy sauce
1 teaspoon sugar
1 teaspoon salt
1 teaspoon monosodium glutamate
2 tablespoons cornstarch
Crisp Chinese noodles

Remove skin and bones from chicken breasts and cut meat into thin lengthwise strips. Cook chicken in oil over high heat until edges are lightly browned. Add all the vegetables and cook, stirring often, for 5 to 7 minutes. Meanwhile, mix together chicken broth, soy sauce, sugar, salt, and monosodium glutamate. Pour over chicken and vegetables, cover, and steam for 5 minutes. Dissolve cornstarch in ¼ cup cold water and stir into skillet until blended and thickened. Serve at once over Chinese noodles. Serves 6.

* When cooking in the Oriental manner, it is best to prepare all the ingredients in advance, since the cooking itself is done very quickly to avoid overcooking the vegetables. This dish requires a large covered skillet or a Chinese wok.

AROUND THE WORLD

ENGLISH ROAST CHICKEN WITH BREAD SAUCE

1 4- to 5-pound roasting chicken
1 teaspoon salt
¼ teaspoon pepper
½ cup melted butter

Wash chicken and pat dry. Sprinkle inside and out with salt and pepper and brush on some of the melted butter. Roast in a shallow pan at 350 degrees for 1½ hours, basting often with melted butter and pan drippings, until nicely browned and tender. Prepare sauce.

BREAD SAUCE:

3 whole cloves
½ medium onion, peeled
1 cup milk
4 peppercorns
½ cup fine dry bread crumbs
2 tablespoons heavy cream
1 tablespoon butter
½ teaspoon salt
Dash paprika

Stick cloves into onion and place in a small saucepan with milk and peppercorns. Simmer over low heat for 8 minutes. Place bread crumbs in a small saucepan, strain milk on top, then stir in cream, butter, salt, and paprika. Heat briefly before serving with chicken. Serves 6.

GOLD COAST CHICKEN STEW

2 fryers, cut up
2 tablespoons salt
1½ cups ground unsalted peanuts
2 medium onions, chopped
2 medium sweet potatoes, peeled and cubed
6 hard-cooked eggs, sliced
4 cups hot cooked rice

Place cleaned chicken pieces into a deep saucepan with 6 cups water and salt. Bring to a boil and cook uncovered over medium heat for ½ hour. Add peanuts, onions, and sweet potatoes and stir well; continue cooking for 1½ hours, adding more salt if necessary. Arrange egg slices on a platter and cover with rice; place chicken and sauce over rice and serve. *Serves 6.*

SOUTH SEAS STEW

½ cup orange juice
2 tablespoons flour
½ cup bottled barbecue sauce
¼ cup packed dark brown sugar
2 tablespoons salad oil

½ teaspoon soy sauce
4 cups diced cooked chicken
1 13-ounce can pineapple chunks, drained
½ cup sliced water chestnuts
Hot cooked white rice
½ cup macadamia nuts

Stir orange juice into flour until smooth. Add barbecue sauce, brown sugar, salad oil, and soy sauce. Place in a 2-quart saucepan and bring to a boil, stirring constantly. When slightly thickened, add chicken, pineapple, and water chestnuts. Reduce heat, cover, and simmer for 10 minutes. Serve over hot rice and sprinkle with macadamia nuts. *Serves 8.*

JAPANESE CHICKEN BUNDLES

2 whole chicken breasts
2 large sweet potatoes
½ pound fresh mushrooms, sliced

1 cup grated mild Cheddar cheese
4 tablespoons softened butter
1 lemon, quartered

Remove skin and bones from chicken breasts and slice. Pare sweet potatoes and cut into strips 1 inch long. Cut 4 12-inch squares each of plastic film and aluminum foil, place film on foil, and spread with half the softened butter. Divide chicken slices among the squares, then mushrooms and sweet potato sticks. Sprinkle with Cheddar cheese and dot lightly with remaining butter. Wrap plastic film tightly, seal foil. Bake at 350 degrees for 25 to 30 minutes or until tender. Serve packets with lemon wedges. *Serves 4.*

CHICKEN ENCHILADAS WITH CHILI SAUCE

3 cups shredded cooked chicken
1 pint sour cream
2 cups shredded Cheddar cheese
2 teaspoons salt
2 4-ounce cans green chili peppers
2 tablespoons olive oil
1 clove garlic, minced
1 1-pound, 12-ounce can stewed tomatoes
2 cups chopped onion
½ teaspoon oregano
½ cup salad oil
12 corn tortillas

Combine chicken, sour cream, Cheddar cheese, and 1 teaspoon salt and set aside. Rinse seeds from chili peppers and sauté in olive oil with garlic. Add tomatoes, onion, 1 teaspoon salt, and oregano and simmer, uncovered, about 30 minutes, or until thick. Meanwhile, heat salad oil in a skillet. Fry each tortilla for 1 minute on each side and drain on paper towels. Divide chicken mixture among them, rolling each tortilla up, and place seam side down in a baking dish. Pour chili sauce over tortillas and bake uncovered at 350 degrees for 20 minutes. *Serves 6.*

GREEK ROAST CHICKEN

4 tablespoons olive oil
3 teaspoons salt
4 tablespoons lemon juice
2 large fryers, split
4 tablespoons butter
2 cups canned peeled tomatoes
1 teaspoon pepper
2 teaspoons oregano

Combine first 3 ingredients and rub into chicken halves on both sides. Place chickens in a roasting pan and cook at 375 degrees for 1 hour, basting frequently with liquid in pan. Melt butter in a saucepan. Add remaining ingredients and simmer for 5 minutes, stirring once or twice. Pour this sauce over the chicken, reduce heat to 350 degrees and continue roasting, basting often, for 1 hour more. *Serves 6.*

CONTINENTAL CHICKEN BREASTS SOUS CLOCHE

4 ounces (1 stick) butter
4 whole chicken breasts
Salt
Pepper
½ pound fresh mushrooms, sliced
¼ teaspoon garlic salt
½ teaspoon crushed tarragon
4 tablespoons dry white wine
½ cup heavy cream

Melt half of the butter in a heavy skillet. Rub chicken breasts with salt and pepper and brown on both sides in the butter. Reduce heat and simmer, covered, for 45 minutes, or until tender. Meanwhile, in another pan, sauté mushrooms in remaining butter, sprinkle on garlic salt and tarragon, and cook over medium heat, stirring occasionally, until mushrooms are tender.

Preheat an ovenproof serving dish with a glass dome. When chicken is done, remove to this platter and arrange mushrooms on top. Keep warm in oven until sauce is made. Add wine to drippings in the pan in which mushrooms were cooked; while wine is boiling rapidly, stir and scrape to clean particles from pan. When liquid is reduced to about 1 tablespoon, add cream and boil until thickened. Remove chicken from oven, pour on sauce, and serve immediately. *Serves 2.*

ITALIAN CHICKEN WITH CAPERS

3 tablespoons flour
2 teaspoons salt
1 teaspoon pepper
2 fryers, cut up
2 medium onions, chopped
4 tablespoons olive oil
1 cup white wine
1 tablespoon tomato paste
1 cup chicken broth
¾ cup garlic wine vinegar
3 anchovies, mashed fine
2 cloves garlic, minced
1 tablespoon drained capers
3 tablespoons chopped sweet pickles
2 tablespoons chopped parsley

Mix flour, salt, and pepper together and rub thoroughly into chickens. Sauté onions in olive oil in a large, heavy skillet for 5 minutes, stirring often. Add chicken pieces and brown well on all sides, then add wine and cook over high heat for 5 minutes. Mix tomato paste and chicken broth and add to chicken, stirring well. Reduce heat, cover pan, and cook 45 minutes. When chicken is ready, boil vinegar for 2 minutes in a small saucepan. Add remaining ingredients and simmer over low heat for 1 minute. Pour over chicken, stir gently, and serve. *Serves 6.*

HOLLANDER'S CHICKEN PIE

2 stewing chickens, cut up
2 tablespoons salt
1¼ teaspoons poultry seasoning
1 teaspoon whole allspice
1 teaspoon whole peppercorns
2 bay leaves
4 small carrots
4 stalks celery, cut in half
2 medium onions, quartered
8 sprigs parsley
4 hard-cooked eggs, sliced
1 ¼-pound slice cooked ham, cubed
2 tablespoons butter
¼ cup flour
2 tablespoons lemon juice
¼ cup dry sherry
¼ teaspoon freshly ground pepper
2 egg yolks plus 1 whole egg
Packaged pie crust mix for 2 9-inch crusts

Place chicken pieces in a large pot and add salt, 1 quart water, 1 teaspoon poultry seasoning, allspice, peppercorns, bay leaves, carrots, celery, onions, and parsley. Cover, bring to a boil, reduce heat, and simmer for 30 minutes. Remove chicken and vegetables with a slotted spoon; strain broth and reserve. Cut carrots and celery into diagonal slices and set aside. Remove skin and bones from chicken, cut into bite-sized pieces, and set aside. In a shallow, large baking dish combine chicken, carrots, celery, eggs, and ham. Melt butter in a medium saucepan, stir in flour, and slowly add 2 cups of the reserved chicken broth, lemon juice, sherry, pepper, and ¼ teaspoon poultry seasoning. Stir until thick and smooth. Beat 2 egg yolks, add a little of the cream sauce, and **stir** back into sauce. Heat, stirring all the while, but do not boil. Pour sauce over chicken.

Prepare pie crust according to package directions. Roll into a rectangle slightly larger than the baking dish, place over chicken, and turn excess under itself to slightly overlap the edge of the dish, making an even line, then scallop edge. Cut decorative slits in the top; cut designs from trimmings and place on crust. Beat whole egg and brush over crust, then bake pie at 425 degrees for 30 minutes, or until crust is done. *Serves 8.*

SPANISH CHICKEN, DUCK, AND SEAFOOD CASSEROLE

- 2 medium onions, chopped
- 2 cloves garlic, minced
- 1 cup olive oil
- 1 3½-pound chicken, cut up
- 1 4-pound duck, cut up
- ½ pound fresh pork, cubed
- 3 chorizos (spanish sausages), sliced
- 1 28-ounce can peeled tomatoes
- 1 green pepper, sliced
- 2 cans beef consommé
- 2 teaspoons salt
- ½ teaspoon saffron
- 1 teaspoon paprika
- 1½ cups long-grain white rice
- ½ pound fresh string beans, cut up
- ½ pound fresh green peas
- 1 cup cauliflower flowerets
- 12 large shrimp, peeled and cleaned
- 1 lobster, cut up
- 1 bouillon cube (optional)

In a large skillet, sauté onions and garlic in ½ cup olive oil for 15 minutes, stirring often. Remove from oil with a slotted spoon and reserve. In the same oil, brown chicken, duck, pork, and chorizos. Place meats in a large casserole and add sautéed onions and garlic, tomatoes, green pepper, consommé, 2 consommé cans of water, salt, saffron, and paprika. Cover and cook slowly for 20 minutes. Brown rice lightly in ½ cup olive oil in the skillet, stirring often. Add to casserole with remaining ingredients, cover, and bake at 350 degrees for 1 hour. If mixture becomes dry, add small amount of broth made with a bouillon cube. *Serves 10.*

HUNGARIAN CHICKEN PAPRIKASH

4 tablespoons butter
4 Bermuda onions, thinly sliced
2 tablespoons paprika
2 fryers, cut up
2 teaspoons salt
¼ teaspoon freshly ground pepper
1 cup canned chicken broth
1 pint sour cream
Hot buttered broad egg noodles

Melt butter in a large ovenproof skillet and sauté onion rings for 5 minutes. Stir in paprika. Sprinkle chicken pieces with salt and pepper and add to skillet; brown on all sides over medium-heat. Stir in chicken broth, cover, and remove to 350-degree oven; bake for 1 hour. Siphon off juices with turkey baster and mix juices with sour cream. Pour sauce over chicken and bake, covered, 10 minutes more. Serve over hot noodles. *Serves 8.*

SWISS CHICKEN-FILLED BRIOCHES

1 large fryer
1 bay leaf
1 tablespoon salt, *more as needed*
1 teaspoon poultry seasoning
⅛ teaspoon nutmeg
1 carrot
2 stalks celery
1 medium onion
2 cloves
1 pound sweetbreads
1 pound lean pork sausage
6 tablespoons butter
½ cup flour
¾ cup dry white wine
2 egg yolks, lightly beaten
½ pint heavy cream
1 tablespoon lemon juice
Pepper to taste
2 4-ounce cans sliced mushrooms, drained
12 brioches (frozen or fresh from the bakery)

In a large saucepan combine chicken, 1½ quarts water, and next 6 ingredients. Pierce onion with cloves and add to chicken. Cover, bring to a boil, and simmer for 1 hour, or until chicken is tender. Meanwhile, wash sweetbreads, place in a bowl with water to cover, and let stand for 1 hour. When chicken is done, remove and cool. Strain broth, discarding vegetables; skim off fat and set broth aside. Remove skin and bones from chicken, dice meat, and set aside. Bring 3 cups of chicken broth to a boil, add sweetbreads, cover, and simmer for 15 minutes. Remove sweetbreads from broth with a slotted spoon, discarding broth, and cool sweetbreads slightly. Cut away membranes; dice meat and set aside. Roll pork sausage into tiny balls and brown thoroughly on all sides in a skillet.

In a saucepan melt butter, stir in flour, and gradually add wine. Add 3 cups of reserved chicken broth, a little at a time, then simmer until thickened. In a bowl combine beaten egg yolks, cream, and lemon juice; season with salt and pepper to taste. When blended, add to wine sauce, then add chicken, sweetbreads, and sausage balls; add drained mushrooms last. Cover and simmer while preparing brioches. Slice tops off brioches and remove most of the dough in the center. Butter the insides and bake at 350 degrees for 5 minutes, then remove from oven. Spoon chicken mixture into brioches, replace tops, and serve. *Serves 12.*

MALAYAN CHICKEN WITH PORK

⅔ cup cider vinegar
2 teaspoons salt
½ teaspoon pepper
4 cloves garlic, sliced
1 bay leaf

1 fryer, cut up
1½ pounds boned pork shoulder
3 tablespoons salad oil
Hot cooked white rice

Mix first 5 ingredients together in a large bowl. Wash and dry chicken pieces; trim all fat from pork and cut into 1½-inch cubes. Toss both meats in vinegar mixture until well coated, and let stand for 30 minutes. Remove meat from marinade, reserving liquid. Heat oil in a deep skillet and brown meats on all sides, than add vinegar mixture and ½ cup water. Simmer, covered, for 30 minutes; remove cover and simmer 15 to 20 minutes longer, or until meats are tender and most of the liquid has evaporated. Serve on hot rice. *Serves 6.*

MAKAHA MOUNTAIN

½ cup flour
1 teaspoon ground ginger
½ teaspoon salt
1 3½-pound fryer, cut up
4 tablespoons butter
1 medium onion, sliced
3 stalks celery, diagonally sliced
1 can condensed cream of chicken soup, undiluted
½ cup chicken broth or bouillon
2 tablespoons soy sauce
2 tablespoons minced drained chutney
1 7-ounce package frozen Chinese snow pea pods (sugar peas), thawed
Crisp Chinese noodles, toasted

Combine flour, ginger, and salt in a bag; shake chicken pieces in bag until well coated. Brown in butter on both sides and place in a buttered baking dish. Sauté onion and celery in remaining drippings until tender; stir in cream of chicken soup, chicken broth, soy sauce, and chutney. Stir, scraping pan, until well heated. Sprinkle snow peas over chicken, then pour on sauce. Cover and bake at 350 degrees for 45 minutes, then uncover and bake 15 minutes more. Serve on mounds of hot crisp noodles. *Serves 4.*

NASI GORENG
(INDONESIAN CHICKEN)

1 4-pound chicken, cut up
Handful parsley sprigs
2 leeks
1 bay leaf
2 tablespoons salt
2 cups uncooked long-grain white rice
4 medium onions, chopped
2 cloves garlic, minced
¼ cup salad oil
1½ cups chopped cooked shrimp
1 cup cooked crab meat
1 cup cubed cooked ham
2 teaspoons ground coriander
1 teaspoon ground cumin seed
½ teaspoon ground dried chili peppers
¼ teaspoon mace
4 tablespoons peanut butter

Place washed chicken in a deep saucepan with 2 quarts water, parsley sprigs, leeks, bay leaf, and 1 tablespoon salt. Cook over medium heat for 1½ hours, or until chicken is tender. Remove chicken and cool slightly; strain the stock and set aside. Remove all meat and cut into strips.

Combine rice, remaining 1 tablespoon salt, and 3½ cups of the stock in a saucepan. Cover and cook over low heat for 20 minutes, then set aside. In a large skillet sauté onions and garlic in oil for 10 minutes, stirring frequently. Add rice and let it brown while stirring occasionally, then add remaining ingredients. Mix gently and allow to heat over low flame for 10 to 15 minutes. *Serves 6.*

SINGAPORE CHICKEN

2 cups shredded coconut
1½ cups half and half
2 tablespoons butter
1 tablespoon ground coriander
1 teaspoon ground anise
¼ teaspoon saffron
1 teaspoon powdered ginger
2 tablespoons grated lemon rind
2 cloves garlic, minced
½ teaspoon ground dried chili peppers
3 tablespoons lemon juice
1 tablespoon plum jam
1 teaspoon sugar
1 tablespoon soy sauce
3 medium onions, sliced
1 large fryer, cut up
Hot cooked white rice

Combine 1½ cups shredded coconut and half and half in a saucepan and bring quickly to a boil; remove from heat and let stand for ½ hour. Strain all liquid from pulp by pressing through a sieve, discarding pulp. Sauté remaining ½ cup coconut in butter until brown. Combine toasted coconut with all remaining ingredients except chicken and rice, and mix well.

Remove all meat from chicken and cut into small cubes. Place meat, spice mixture, and coconut cream in a skillet. Cook over high heat, stirring constantly, until mixture begins to boil. Reduce heat, cover, and cook for 10 to 15 minutes. Remove chicken from sauce and place on a bed of rice then pour sauce on top. *Serves 6.*

AROUND THE WORLD

INDIAN CHICKEN KORMA

2 fryers, cut up
1 cup yogurt
4 cloves garlic, minced
2 medium onions, minced
½ teaspoon powdered ginger
½ teaspoon ground cloves
1½ teaspoons salt
4 tablespoons butter
1 tablespoon curry powder
1 teaspoon ground almonds
Hot cooked white rice

Wash and dry chicken pieces and place in a large bowl. Combine yogurt with half the garlic and spread over chicken. Let stand at room temperature for 2 hours, basting occasionally. In a large pan, sauté remaining garlic, onions, ginger, cloves, and salt in butter for 5 minutes. Add curry powder and almonds and continue to cook 5 minutes more, stirring all the while. Add chicken and yogurt sauce, mixing well. Cover and cook slowly for 2 hours, stirring occasionally. Serve with rice. *Serves 6.*

NORTH AFRICAN COUSCOUS

2 cups "bulgur" (tiny wheat pellets, found at Near Eastern food stores)
4 teaspoons salt
8 ounces (2 sticks) butter
3 medium onions, chopped
1 5-pound chicken, cut up
2 pounds lamb, cubed
2 green peppers, sliced
2 carrots, sliced
3 tomatoes, cubed
1 teaspoon pepper
½ teaspoon cayenne pepper
2 cups drained canned chick-peas
½ 10-ounce package frozen green peas
1 cup cubed yellow squash
6 canned artichoke hearts

In a large bowl, combine bulgur, 2 cups water, and 1 teaspoon salt, mixing well. Rub bulgur between hands above bowl, letting it drop back repeatedly. Be careful not to make lumps. Repeat several times, then allow bulgur to soak until all the water is absorbed.

In a large, deep saucepan, melt 1 stick of butter and brown

onions, chicken, and lamb. Add just enough water to cover, then add green peppers, carrots, tomatoes, 3 teaspoons salt, peppers, and cayenne pepper. Placing the bulgur in a large colander over the chicken, cover pot as tightly as possible and simmer for 1½ hours. Add chick-peas, green peas, squash, and artichoke hearts to chicken and continue to cook, covered, for 45 minutes. Place bulgur in a bowl. Melt remaining stick of butter, add to bulgur, stirring with a fork, and place bulgur in center of a platter. Surround with chicken and vegetables. *Serves 6.*

PAKISTANI BAKED CHICKEN

2 whole roasting chickens
3 teaspoons garlic puree
2 medium onions, grated
½ teaspoon ground dried chili peppers
½ teaspoon ground cloves
1½ teaspoons salt
1 teaspoon pepper
¼ teaspoon ground cardamon seed
½ teaspoon powdered ginger
½ cup ground blanched almonds
4 tablespoons melted butter

Peel all skin from chickens very carefully, then prick meat with a dinner fork. Mix all remaining ingredients into a paste with 2 tablespoons water and spread over all surfaces of chickens, including insides. Place chickens in a roasting pan and bake uncovered at 350 degrees for 1½ hours. If chicken should stick to pan, add a little water. *Serves 6.*

PERSIAN JOOJEH

1 cup cracked wheat
5 ounces (1¼ sticks) butter
1 1-pound can chick-peas, drained
1 cup slivered blanched toasted almonds
Salt
Pepper
1 4-pound roasting chicken
½ cup hot chicken broth

AROUND THE WORLD

Cook cracked wheat in 1 cup water over low heat for ½ hour. Add ¼ stick butter and cook 10 minutes more, or until tender. Combine with chick-peas, almonds, 2 teaspoons salt, and ½ teaspoon pepper, tossing well. Rub chicken inside and out with more salt and pepper. Spoon stuffing into body cavities and skewer shut. Place in a roasting pan and cook at 300 degrees for 2 to 2½ hours, or until well browned and tender, basting often with chicken broth combined with 1 stick melted butter. *Serves 6.*

PHILIPPINE ADOBO

1 cup shredded coconut
1 fryer, boned and cubed
2 pounds boneless pork, cubed
¼ cup olive oil
3 teaspoons garlic puree
1 tablespoon salt
1 teaspoon pepper
2 bay leaves, crumbled
½ can beef consommé
½ cup wine vinegar
Hot cooked white rice

Combine coconut and 1 cup water in a saucepan. Bring to a rapid boil, remove from flame, and set aside for ½ hour. Press all the liquid from the coconut into a bowl and discard the pulp. Sauté chicken and pork cubes in olive oil, a few at a time, until all are well browned. Add next 6 ingredients, cover, and simmer for 1 hour, stirring occasionally. Add coconut water and continue cooking for 10 minutes. Correct seasoning; serve over rice. *Serves 6.*

SCOTCH STOVIES

1 fryer, cut up
6 tablespoons butter
4 large potatoes, pared and sliced
2 teaspoons salt
2 large onions, peeled and thinly sliced
¼ teaspoon garlic powder
¼ teaspoon pepper
1 cup chicken broth

Brown chicken pieces in 3 tablespoons butter in a large skillet, then take half of the chicken out of the pan. Place half of the potatoes and onions over chicken in pan, sprinkle on half of the seasoning, and dot with 1½ tablespoons butter. Place remaining chicken back in pan and cover with remaining potatoes, onions, and seasoning; dot with remaining 1½ tablespoons butter. Pour on the chicken broth, bring to a boil, reduce heat, and cover tightly. Simmer for 1 hour. *Serves 4.*

SUPRÊMES DE POULET

POTATOES:

¾ cup melted butter
8 medium potatoes, pared, cooked, and mashed

3 egg yolks, beaten
Warm milk

Add ½ cup melted butter to mashed potatoes and stir in egg yolks. If too dry, add warm milk to moisten. Spoon all but 1½ cups of the potatoes in a tall mound in the center of a large heat-proof platter, and smooth with a spatula. Spoon remaining potatoes into a pastry tube with a star tip, and decorate mound with swirls. Brush with remaining melted butter and bake uncovered in a 425-degree oven for 20 minutes. Meanwhile, prepare chicken.

CHICKEN:

4 whole chicken breasts
4 tablespoons flour
Salt
Freshly ground pepper
4 tablespoons butter
1 cup chicken broth
½ teaspoon rosemary

½ teaspoon seasoned salt
½ cup Sauterne
Mushroom caps, sautéed in butter
Parsley sprigs
2 tablespoons flour

Remove skin from chicken breasts cut in half, and remove bones. Dust lightly with flour seasoned with salt and pepper and brown well in butter on all sides. Remove from pan and keep warm. Add chicken broth, rosemary, seasoned salt, ¼ teaspoon pepper, and Sauterne to pan, stirring to loosen particles. Replace chicken in pan, reduce heat to low, and simmer, covered, for 15 minutes.

Place chicken around mound of potatoes on serving platter and decorate with sautéed mushroom caps and parsley sprigs. Serve pan juices as sauce or thicken with flour and 2 tablespoons water for gravy. *Serves 8.*

UKRANIAN CHICKEN IN SOUR CREAM

2 large fryers, cut up
3 teaspoons salt
1 teaspoon pepper
¾ cup flour

2 eggs
1½ cups bread crumbs
4 ounces (1 stick) butter
3 cups sour cream

Wash and dry chicken pieces. Combine 2 teaspoons salt, ½ teaspoon pepper, and flour in a paper bag and lightly coat chicken pieces. Beat eggs with 3 tablespoons water in a bowl; dip chicken in egg, then in bread crumbs. Melt half the butter in a skillet and brown chicken, adding more butter as it is needed. Place chicken in a baking dish; sprinkle with 1 teaspoon salt and ½ teaspoon pepper and bake uncovered at 375 degrees for 30 minutes. Pour half the sour cream over the chicken and continue to bake for 20 minutes, then add remaining sour cream and bake 20 minutes more. *Serves 6.*

NORTH AFRICAN ROAST CHICKEN

5 teaspoons salt
1½ teaspoons pepper
2 large roasting chickens, with livers and gizzards
4 ounces (1 stick) butter
3 medium onions, finely chopped

3 tablespoons chopped parsley
2 hard-cooked eggs, chopped
1 cup pistachio nuts
½ cup seedless raisins

Combine 3 teaspoons salt and 1 teaspoon pepper and rub into chickens, inside and out. Set aside. Melt butter in a saucepan and

AROUND THE WORLD

sauté onions for 10 minutes. Grind chicken livers and gizzards very fine in a food chopper and add to onions; continue to cook for another 10 minutes, stirring often. Add remaining ingredients, 2 teaspoons salt, and ½ teaspoon pepper, and mix well. Spoon into chicken and close openings with skewers. Roast at 350 degrees for 2 hours, basting frequently with pan drippings. *Serves 6.*

ORANGE CHICKEN FROM ECUADOR

2 cups orange juice
1 cup finely minced onions
½ teaspoon crushed Mexican red peppers
1 bay leaf
2 small broiler-fryers, cut up
4 tablespoons butter
2 teaspoons salt
2 tablespoons flour
½ teaspoon sugar
2 oranges, sliced thin

In a large pottery bowl combine orange juice, onions, red peppers, and bay leaf and mix well. Place chicken in marinade and stir until evenly coated. Refrigerate overnight, basting occasionally. About 1½ hours before serving remove chicken pieces, reserving marinade. Melt butter in a large ovenproof dish and brown chicken. Sprinkle with salt, flour, and sugar and stir until flour is browned. Add marinade, cover, and bake in a 325-degree oven for 1 hour. Garnish with orange slices and serve. *Serves 4.*

SOUTH AMERICAN POLLO ASADO

1 3-pound fryer, cut up
⅓ cup olive oil
1 cup sliced onion
1 cup sliced carrots
1 cup sliced mushrooms
4 tablespoons butter
1 tablespoon chopped chives
1½ teaspoons salt
¼ teaspoon pepper
⅛ teaspoon mace (optional)
4 tablespoons flour
1½ cups dry white wine
1 hard-cooked egg, sliced
Several sprigs parsley
Hot steamed white rice

Brown chicken in olive oil in a large skillet. Meanwhile, in another skillet, sauté onion, carrots, and mushrooms in butter for 10 to 12 minutes, or until tender. Add chives, salt, pepper, and mace if desired. Stir in flour and cook 1 minute, stirring well, then blend in wine. Pour this mixture over the chicken, cover, and simmer for 45 minutes. Place in a heated serving dish, garnish with egg slices and parsley, and serve accompanied by steamed rice. *Serves 4.*

13

WINEBIBBER'S CORNER

CHICKEN VÉRONIQUE

- 1 3-pound broiler-fryer, quartered
- 3 tablespoons butter
- 1 teaspoon salt
- ¼ teaspoon pepper
- 3 tablespoons flour
- ¼ teaspoon crushed rosemary leaves
- ¼ teaspoon crushed bay leaf
- ¼ teaspoon dried thyme leaves
- ¼ teaspoon garlic puree
- 1 cup chicken broth
- ⅔ cup Sauterne
- 2 cups halved seedless green grapes

Brown chicken quarters in butter on both sides in a large skillet, then remove from pan. Sprinkle with salt and pepper. Add flour to drippings and stir for a few minutes; add seasonings and stir in chicken broth, Sauterne, and half of the grapes. Bring to a boil, stirring constantly, then add chicken. Reduce heat to a simmer, cover, and cook for 45 minutes, or until chicken is tender. Remove chicken to a platter and keep warm. Strain gravy, discarding cooked grapes. Return gravy to pan, add remaining grapes, and heat briefly. Pour gravy over chicken. *Serves 4.*

WINEBIBBER'S CORNER

APPLEJACK CHICKEN

1 3-pound broiler-fryer, quartered
4 ounces (1 stick) butter
4 ounces applejack brandy
3 Gravenstein apples, pared, cored, and sliced

Wash chicken quarters and pat dry. Melt butter in a large heavy skillet and brown chicken on all sides. Remove from heat. Heat 3 ounces of brandy, pour on chicken, and ignite. When brandy has stopped burning, return skillet to low heat and spread apple slices over chicken. Cover tightly and simmer for 40 minutes, checking occasionally to see that the chicken is not sticking. If it is, add 1 tablespoon water. Add the last ounce of brandy, cover, and cook 10 minutes more. *Serves 4.*

CHICKEN MARCHAND DE VIN

1 3-pound broiling chicken, split and quartered
Flour
6 tablespoons butter
¾ cup minced shallots or green onions
3 cloves garlic, finely minced
½ cup finely minced fresh mushrooms
½ cup finely minced cooked ham
⅛ teaspoon cayenne pepper
2 beef bouillon cubes
½ cup claret

Wash and drain chicken quarters and dust with flour. Melt butter in a skillet and gently brown chicken on both sides; remove and place in a shallow covered baking dish, reserving butter. Bake in a 325-degree oven for 30 minutes. Meanwhile, reheat reserved butter in skillet and sauté shallots, garlic, mushrooms, and ham. When the vegetables are tender, stir in 2 tablespoons flour and cayenne pepper. Dissolve bouillon cubes in ¾ cup boiling water; stir into skillet with claret, blending until smooth. Cover and simmer for 15 minutes, stirring occasionally. Uncover baking dish, pour sauce over chicken, and continue to bake, uncovered, for 20 minutes. *Serves 4.*

BRANDIED CHICKEN SHELL

1 5-pound roasting chicken, cut up
4 ounces (1 stick) butter
1 ounce brandy
1 Bermuda onion, thinly sliced
1½ teaspoons salt
¼ teaspoon pepper
1 tablespoon curry powder
1 cup heavy cream
Crisp lettuce
Lemon wedges

Wash chicken parts and dry thoroughly. Melt butter in a large, heavy iron skillet and gently brown chicken pieces, a few at a time, until all are golden on both sides. Return all chicken pieces to pan, then warm the brandy, pour over the chicken, and ignite. When flame has gone out, sprinkle onion slices, salt, and pepper over chicken. Add ½ cup water, cover, and simmer for 1¼ hours, or until chicken is ready to fall away from the bones. Blend curry powder into sauce, baste chicken well, then remove chicken from skillet. When it is cool enough to handle, remove skin and bones and cut breasts into strips. Place strips in the bottom of a 9- or 10-inch shell mold, cover with remaining meat, and set aside. Stir cream into drippings in pan; heat but do not boil. Press sauce through a sieve onto the chicken; cool, cover, and refrigerate until set. Unmold by placing in hot water for a few seconds. Serve on crisp lettuce with lemon wedges. *Serves 6.*

COSTA RICAN CHICKEN IN CIDER

2 fryers, cut up
2 teaspoons salt
1 teaspoon pepper
4 ounces (1 stick) butter
3 medium onions, chopped
2 cloves garlic, minced
2 green peppers, sliced fine
¼ teaspoon ground dried chili peppers
2 cups hard cider
3 tablespoons vinegar
12 prunes, soaked in water
12 stuffed olives
12 small white onions
4 medium potatoes, peeled and cubed
3 chorizos (Spanish sausages)

WINEBIBBER'S CORNER

Rub chicken pieces with salt and pepper, then brown in butter with chopped onions in a heavy skillet. Add garlic, green peppers, chili peppers, cider, and vinegar. Cover and simmer for 1 hour. Add all remaining ingredients except chorizos and continue cooking. Meanwhile, cut chorizos into small slices and fry in a separate skillet for 5 minutes. Drain and add to chicken; cook for 10 minutes more. *Serves 6.*

SAUTÉED CHICKEN LIVERS IN WINE SAUCE

2 pounds chicken livers	4 ounces (1 stick) butter
1 cup flour	1 teaspoon oregano
1 teaspoon salt	1 teaspoon rosemary
¼ teaspoon pepper	1 cup Riesling

Shake chicken livers with flour, salt, and pepper in a paper bag until well coated. Melt butter in a skillet until bubbly; brown livers quickly on all sides, then spoon off excess drippings. Sprinkle on oregano and rosemary and reduce heat. Pour in Riesling and ½ cup water and simmer, covered, for 45 minutes. Add more water if necessary to keep from sticking. *Serves 6.*

MELLOW CHICKEN SAUTÉ

4 whole chicken legs and thighs	½ clove garlic, minced
4 ounces (1 stick) butter	1 teaspoon salt
¼ cup chopped green onion	1 cup dry vermouth
	3 tablespoons brandy

Brown chicken in butter with green onion and garlic. When chicken is golden on both sides, sprinkle with salt and pour on vermouth and brandy. Cover, reduce heat, and simmer for 25 to 30 minutes, or until fork-tender. Serve chicken covered with wine sauce. *Serves 4.*

CHICKEN WITH ARTICHOKES ROSÉ

1 3-pound broiler-fryer, quartered
Dixie Fry
7 tablespoons butter
1 9-ounce package frozen artichoke hearts
¼ cup chopped green onion
½ cup chopped fresh mushrooms
2 tablespoons flour
¾ cup chicken broth
¾ cup rosé wine

Shake chicken quarters in a bag with Dixie Fry. Melt 4 tablespoons butter in a shallow baking dish and place chicken, skin side down, in the buttered dish. Bake at 375 degrees for 45 minutes. Cook artichoke hearts according to package directions; drain and place around baked chicken. Melt remaining butter in a small skillet and sauté onion and mushrooms for 3 minutes. Stir in flour, chicken broth, and rosé wine, and simmer, stirring, for 3 minutes. Pour over chicken and artichokes. Reduce heat to 325 degrees and bake 20 minutes more. *Serves 4.*

COMPOTE OF CHICKEN MARSALA

3 chicken breasts, halved
6 tablespoons butter
1 1-pound can tiny potatoes, drained
½ pound fresh small button mushrooms
2 10-ounce packages frozen peas with pearl onions, partially defrosted
3 tablespoons flour
2 cups light cream
1 cup Marsala
1 teaspoon salt
¼ teaspoon pepper
¼ teaspoon sage

Brown chicken breasts on all sides in 4 tablespoons butter, and remove to a baking dish. In the same butter brown the potatoes lightly and add to chicken. Sauté mushrooms in remaining drippings and add to chicken, along with peas and onions. Add 2 tablespoons butter to remaining drippings, stir in flour, then blend in cream, stirring until bubbling and thickened. Slowly stir in Marsala and seasonings, and let simmer for 3 minutes. Pour over chicken and vegetables; bake at 375 degrees for 1 hour. *Serves 6.*

WINEBIBBER'S CORNER

VINEYARD CHICKEN

4 chicken legs and thighs	8 tablespoons butter
¼ cup flour	1 cup Chablis
1 teaspoon garlic salt	¼ cup sliced green onion
¼ teaspoon pepper	8 mushrooms, sliced
½ teaspoon crumbled dried rosemary	2 tablespoons finely minced parsley

Shake chicken parts in a paper bag that contains flour, garlic salt, pepper, and rosemary. Melt 6 tablespoons butter in a heavy skillet and brown chicken well on all sides. Pour Chablis over chicken, reduce heat to low, cover tightly, and simmer for 20 minutes. Meanwhile, sauté onion and mushrooms in remaining 2 tablespoons butter in a small skillet until tender. Add to chicken at the end of the 20 minutes, cover, and cook 15 minutes longer. There shouldn't be much gravy. Sprinkle with parsley and serve. *Serves 4.*

WINEBIBBER'S CHICKEN

3 pounds meaty chicken parts (no wings or backs)	1 cup milk
11 tablespoons butter	½ cup Chablis
1½ teaspoons salt	⅓ cup white port
¼ teaspoon pepper	¼ cup brandy
3 tablespoons flour	1 pint half and half
	Hot prepared wild rice

Wipe chicken pieces with damp paper towel. Using 4 tablespoons butter, brown chicken on both sides in a large skillet. Sprinkle with salt and pepper. Add 4 tablespoons butter, reduce heat to a simmer, cover, and cook ½ hour. Meanwhile, prepare a cream sauce with 3 tablespoons butter, flour, and milk, stirring until thickened. Simmer 1 minute and set aside. When chicken is done, remove from pan. Add Chablis, port, and brandy to skillet and bring to a boil, stirring all the while. Lower heat and simmer 5 minutes to reduce liquid. Blend in cream sauce and half and half, then return chicken to pan and simmer for 5 minutes. Serve over wild rice. *Serves 6.*

SPICY CHICKEN IN RED WINE

2 fryers, cut up
¾ cup flour
1 tablespoon salt
½ teaspoon pepper
½ cup olive oil
3 medium onions, thickly sliced
3 tomatoes, chopped
½ pound mushrooms, sliced
2 green peppers, sliced
1½ cups red wine
½ teaspoon chili powder
½ teaspoon oregano
1 bay leaf

Dust chicken pieces lightly in flour seasoned with salt and pepper. Brown on all sides in olive oil in a large skillet. Add all remaining ingredients, cover skillet tightly, and simmer for 1 hour. Remove bay leaf before serving. *Serves 6.*

14
GAME HENS

ISLAND GAME HENS

1 cup uncooked brown rice
2 cups chicken broth
½ cup diced celery
½ cup sliced macadamia nuts
7 tablespoons butter
1 cup drained crushed pineapple
1 tablespoon minced green onion
¼ teaspoon poultry seasoning
Dash nutmeg
4 Rock Cornish game hens
¼ cup dry vermouth
¼ teaspoon ground ginger

Add brown rice to boiling chicken broth. Reduce heat, cover, and steam for 20 minutes. Meanwhile, sauté celery and macadamia nuts in 3 tablespoons butter for 8 minutes. When rice is done, add celery-nut mixture, well-drained pineapple, green onion, poultry seasoning, and nutmeg; toss lightly. Place this stuffing in cavities of hens, skewer closed, and place on a shallow baking dish. Melt remaining 4 tablespoons butter, combine with vermouth and ginger, and baste hens. Bake at 350 degrees for 1 hour, basting 3 or 4 times. *Serves 4.*

GAME HENS

FAR EASTERN STEAMED GAME HENS

1 teaspoon salt
2 Rock Cornish game hens
1 clove garlic
3 tablespoons honey
3 tablespoons soy sauce
¼ teaspoon garlic powder
1 tablespoon sake or dry sherry
4 servings prepared chicken fried rice
2 tablespoons chopped green onion

Rub salt inside and out into washed and dried hens. Add garlic clove to 1-inch-deep boiling water in a large saucepan. Place hens on a wire rack over water; cover and steam for ½ hour. Remove hens and cut in half; place in a buttered baking dish. Combine honey, soy sauce, sake, and garlic powder. Brush hens generously and bake for 20 minutes in a 425-degree oven, basting every 5 minutes. Place on hot fried rice and sprinkle with green onion. Serves 4.

FLAMING ROAST GAME HEN WITH CHERRIES

4 Rock Cornish game hens
1½ teaspoons salt, more if necessary
¼ teaspoon pepper, more if necessary
½ cup melted butter
1 cup red wine
1 17-ounce can pitted black cherries
2 tablespoons cornstarch
¼ cup brandy

Sprinkle hens inside and out with salt and pepper. Set in a shallow baking dish, brush with some of the melted butter, and roast at 350 degrees for 50 minutes. Meanwhile heat wine in a small saucepan. Drain cherries, reserving ¼ cup cherry juice. Dissolve cornstarch in the cherry juice; add to hot wine and stir until slightly thickened and clear. Add drained cherries, heat briefly, reduce heat, and keep warm. When hens are done, cut each in half. Dip in remaining melted butter, sprinkle with more salt and pepper if necessary, and place in one layer, skin side up, in a flameproof serving dish or skillet. Pour cherry sauce over hens, and reheat briefly, then remove from heat. Warm brandy, pour over hens, and ignite. Serve immediately. *Serves 4.*

GAME HENS WITH WILD RICE STUFFING

2 cups cooked wild rice
¼ cup minced onion
¼ cup minced celery
¼ cup minced mushrooms
½ clove garlic, minced
5 tablespoons butter

6 tablespoons dry white wine
2 Rock Cornish game hens
½ teaspoon salt
Cooked fresh peas
Stuffed mushroom caps

Cook wild rice according to package directions. Sauté onion, celery, mushrooms, and garlic in 3 tablespoons butter for 5 minutes. Add to rice and blend in 4 tablespoons wine. Wash hens and pat dry. Sprinkle with salt. Fill cavities with wild rice stuffing and close openings with skewers. Melt remaining 2 tablespoons butter and 2 tablespoons wine together, baste hens, and roast, basting often, at 350 degrees for 50 minutes, or until tender. Serve topped with pan juices and accompanied by cooked fresh peas and stuffed mushroom caps. *Serves 2.*

GERMAN GAME HENS WITH SAUERKRAUT

2 Rock Cornish game hens
¼ teaspoon salt
Dash pepper
4 strips bacon
6 tablespoons butter
2 carrots
4 small white onions, peeled

1 juniper berry, crushed
½ cup sour cream
1½ cups canned sauerkraut
1 teaspoon sugar
¾ cup dry white wine
Mashed potatoes

GAME HENS

Rub hens with salt and pepper. Tie 2 strips bacon around each breast. Brown on all sides in 4 tablespoons butter in a deep skillet. Cut carrots diagonally into 1-inch pieces and add to skillet. Add onions and juniper berry. Cover and simmer, turning occasionally, for 30 to 40 minutes, adding a little hot water if necessary to prevent sticking. When hens are tender, stir sour cream into pan drippings. Meanwhile, rinse and drain sauerkraut thoroughly. Sauté in 2 tablespoons butter for 5 minutes. Add sugar and wine and cook over low heat, covered, for 30 minutes. Place sauerkraut on a heated platter and set game hens on top. Cover with sour cream gravy and serve with mashed potatoes. *Serves 2.*

COLD BRANDIED GAME HENS WITH PEACHES

2 Rock Cornish game hens
Salt
Pepper
Paprika
1 pickled peach, sliced
2 tablespoons peach syrup
2 tablespoons melted butter
6 tablespoons brandy

Sprinkle game hens inside and out with salt, pepper, and paprika. Spoon peach slices into body cavities and skewer shut. Combine peach syrup with melted butter and keep warm; brush on game hens. Bake hens at 350 degrees, basting often, for 50 minutes, or until tender. Warm brandy, pour over hens, and light immediately. Cool hens and wrap in aluminum foil or plastic film until ready to serve. *Serves 2.*

PICNIC GAME HENS

6 frozen Rock Cornish game hens, thawed
2 teaspoons salt
¼ teaspoon pepper
1 teaspoon dried basil
1 teaspoon dried rosemary
¼ cup melted butter
¾ cup warm Sauterne
Cherry tomatoes
Pickle chips
Mild Cheddar cheese cubes
Pitted ripe olives

Wash hens and pat dry. Rub inside and out with mixture of salt, pepper, basil, and rosemary. Place several inches apart in a baking dish and brush with combined butter and Sauterne. Bake in a 400-degree oven for 45 minutes. Keep basting sauce warm and brush on every 6 to 8 minutes. When hens are tender, remove to large squares of aluminum foil to cool. Cut hens in half. Using large toothpicks, prepare 2 skewers of cherry tomatoes, pickle chips, cheese cubes, and olives for each hen. Wrap in plastic film and place between halves of each hen. Wrap reassembled hens tightly in aluminum foil and take to the picnic. *Serves 6.*

POTTED GAME HENS WITH VEGETABLES

- 6 slices bacon
- 2 Rock Cornish game hens, halved
- ¼ cup flour
- 1 teaspoon salt
- ¼ teaspoon pepper
- 1 cup sliced fresh mushrooms
- 2 tablespoons chopped parsley
- ½ cup chicken broth
- 1 bay leaf
- 1 cup red wine
- 8 small onions, peeled
- 4 small carrots, pared and sliced
- 2 cups fresh or frozen peas

Cook bacon in a large skillet until crisp. Remove from pan, drain and crumble, and place in a baking dish. Wash hen halves and pat dry. Combine flour, salt, and pepper in a paper bag and shake hens in bag until well dusted. Reserve seasoned flour. Brown hens on both sides in bacon drippings and remove to baking dish. Sauté mushrooms and parsley in remaining drippings for 5 minutes and add to baking dish. Stir remaining seasoned flour into drippings; add chicken broth and heat to a boil, scraping loose any particles sticking to pan. Add bay leaf and simmer, stirring, until thickened. Remove bay leaf, stir in wine, and heat. Place onions and carrots around chicken. Pour on wine sauce, cover, and bake 45 minutes at 350 degrees. Add peas and bake 15 minutes more. *Serves 4.*

GAME HENS

BUTTER-BARBECUED GAME HENS

4 Rock Cornish game hens
1 1-pound can small onions
6 ounces (1½ sticks) butter
1 teaspoon garlic puree
2 tablespoons lemon juice
1 tablespoon soy sauce
½ teaspoon thyme
½ teaspoon oregano
½ teaspoon paprika
¼ teaspoon freshly ground pepper

Rinse game hens and pat dry. Drain onions and toss with 2 ounces melted butter. Divide onions among the cavities of the hens, skewer openings, and truss legs and wings. Place on a rotisserie skewer when coals are medium-hot. Meanwhile, prepare basting sauce by melting the remaining stick of butter with garlic, then adding remaining ingredients. Place a drip-pan under the chicken and baste generously with butter sauce while rotating for 50 to 60 minutes, or until drumsticks move easily. *Serves 4.*

GAME HENS RAPHAEL WEILL

½ lemon, plus ½ teaspoon lemon juice
4 Rock Cornish game hens, halved
1½ teaspoons salt
¼ teaspoon pepper
4 tablespoons butter
¼ teaspoon garlic puree
¼ cup minced parsley
½ cup dry white wine
½ teaspoon chicken bouillon granules
4 egg yolks
1 cup heavy cream

Rub ½ lemon into hen halves, releasing its juice. Sprinkle with salt and pepper on both sides. Place butter, garlic puree, and parsley in a skillet and lightly brown hens on both sides. Reduce heat, cover, and simmer for 15 minutes, shaking frequently to prevent sticking. Add wine. Dissolve bouillon in 2 tablespoons boiling water and add. Simmer, covered, 10 to 15 minutes longer, or until fork-tender. Meanwhile, beat together egg yolks and cream. When hens are done remove to a warm platter. Pour egg mixture into pan and stirring constantly over lowest flame, heat until sauce thickens. Add ½ teaspoon lemon juice. Remove hens to a serving dish and cover with cream sauce. *Serves 4.*

15
SALADS

CHICKEN BREASTS IN ASPIC

6 whole boned chicken breasts
4 14-ounce cans chicken broth
2 envelopes unflavored gelatin
1 egg white, lightly beaten
1 cup sour cream
¼ teaspoon finely crumbled tarragon leaves
Crisp lettuce leaves
3 avocados, sliced
Lemon juice

Place chicken breasts and chicken broth in a saucepan and bring to a boil. Cover, reduce heat to a simmer, and cook for ½ hour, or until chicken is tender. Lift meat from broth and carefully remove skin; cut breasts in half, cover, and refrigerate. Strain broth through a fine sieve, cool, and remove fat. Strain once more. There should be about 6 cups of broth. Soak gelatin in ½ cup cold water for 5 minutes. Add egg white to broth in a saucepan, and using a wire whisk, stir constantly while bringing broth to a rolling boil. Remove broth from heat and let cool for 5 minutes. Stir in gelatin until completely dissolved. Stir in sour cream and tarragon and refrigerate until mixture has just begun to set, then

SALADS

remove from refrigerator. Place chicken breasts in a shallow dish so that pieces are close together but do not touch. Pour gelatin mixture over them and return to refrigerator to set until firm. Cut squares of aspic and place on beds of lettuce leaves. Surround with avocado slices sprinkled with lemon juice. *Serves 6.*

PACIFICA SALAD

2 cups cubed cooked chicken
1 cup seedless grapes
½ cup chopped celery
½ cup chopped chutney
½ cup pine nuts
½ cup sliced water chestnuts

Combine all ingredients and chill. Prepare dressing.

DRESSING:

1 cup sour cream
2 tablespoons brown sugar
½ teaspoon salt
Juice of 1 lemon
2 tablespoons grated onion

Combine all ingredients and chill. Pour over salad. *Serves 6.*

PÂTÉ SALAD MOLD

1 tablespoon unflavored gelatin
2 cups boiling beef broth
1 8-ounce package cream cheese
2 tablespoons light cream
⅛ teaspoon garlic powder
½ teaspoon Beau Monde seasoning or seasoned salt
½ cup mashed chicken livers
2 teaspoons butter
2 teaspoons grated onion

Soften gelatin in ¼ cup cold water, then dissolve in boiling beef broth. Soften cream cheese with cream, then add garlic powder and Beau Monde seasoning. Sauté chicken livers in butter with onion; cool. Pour half the gelatin into a 8-inch ring mold that has been rinsed in cold water, and chill until firm. Combine remaining gelatin with cream cheese and chicken livers and smooth on top. Chill until firm. *Serves 8.*

CHICKEN-ALMOND SALAD

2 cups finely diced cooked chicken
¼ cup Italian salad dressing
½ cup toasted slivered blanched almonds
½ cup finely diced celery
2 teaspoons chopped capers
½ cup mayonnaise
1½ teaspoons lemon juice
½ teaspoon salt
Dash white pepper
Crisp lettuce

Marinate chicken in salad dressing for 1 hour. Drain thoroughly. Combine chicken with next 7 ingredients in order listed and toss well. Serve on beds of crisp lettuce. *Serves 4.*

CHICKEN SALAD WITH GREEN GODDESS DRESSING

1 4-pound stewing chicken
1 stalk celery
1 carrot
1 medium onion, peeled and quartered
Several sprigs parsley
1 tablespoon salt
1 bay leaf
½ teaspoon poultry seasoning

Place all ingredients in a large saucepan and add water to barely cover the chicken. Cover, bring to a boil, reduce heat, and simmer until tender. Allow chicken to cool in broth, then remove. Skin, bone, and dice the meat into ¼-inch cubes. Strain broth and save for other uses. Prepare dressing.

DRESSING:

3 tablespoons finely minced parsley
3 tablespoons finely minced watercress
1 ripe avocado, mashed
3 green onions, finely minced
¼ cup finely chopped celery
1 cup mayonnaise
4 anchovy fillets, minced
1 tablespoon tarragon vinegar
Crisp lettuce leaves
Tomato wedges

Combine ingredients in order and mix well. Add to cubed chicken and blend. Serve on lettuce leaves ringed with tomato wedges. *Serves 8.*

SALADS

CHICKEN AND VEGETABLE SALAD

- 3 cups diced cooked chicken
- 1 12-ounce can kernel corn, drained
- 6 tomatoes, cubed
- 3 green peppers, minced
- 3 cups mayonnaise
- 2 teaspoons salt
- ½ teaspoon pepper
- ¼ teaspoon chili powder
- 6 large lettuce leaves, washed and chilled
- 6 hard-cooked eggs, sliced

Combine chicken, corn, tomatoes, green peppers, 1 cup mayonnaise, and seasonings, mixing thoroughly. Set lettuce leaves on 6 salad plates; divide chicken mixture among them and pat into smooth, flat rounds. Coat servings with remaining mayonnaise, then cover with egg slices. Chill 1 hour before serving. *Serves 6.*

FROSTED CHICKEN BREAST SALAD

- 4 whole chicken breasts
- 1 14-ounce can chicken broth
- 1 3-ounce package cream cheese
- 3 tablespoons mayonnaise
- 1 teaspoon lemon juice
- ¼ teaspoon grated lemon peel
- ¼ teaspoon salt
- 2 tablespoons snipped chives
- Crisp lettuce leaves
- 2 tomatoes, sliced
- Seasoned salt
- 1 avocado, sliced

On the morning of the day the salad is to be served, remove bones and skin from chicken breasts and simmer in broth for 30 minutes, or until tender. Cool, then refrigerate, leaving meat in the broth. About ½ hour before serving time, drain and dry chicken, saving broth for soup or gravy.

Mix cream cheese, mayonnaise, lemon juice, lemon peel, salt, and 1 tablespoon chives until mixture is creamy. Spread on all sides of chicken breasts. Arrange lettuce leaves and tomato slices on 4 salad plates and sprinkle with seasoned salt. Place 1 frosted chicken breast on each plate, sprinkle with remaining 1 tablespoon chives, and garnish with avocado slices. *Serves 4.*

HOT CHICKEN SALAD

3 cups diced cooked chicken
1 cup sliced celery
1 3-ounce can ripe olives, drained and sliced
1 tablespoon minced onion
1 teaspoon salt
1 cup shredded sharp Cheddar cheese
1 cup mayonnaise
1 cup crushed potato chips
1 tomato

Combine chicken, celery, olives, onion, salt, and ½ cup Cheddar cheese. Fold in mayonnaise and turn mixture into a 1½-quart baking dish. Sprinkle on remaining cheese, then potato chips. Cut tomato into 6 wedges and distribute them over the top. Bake uncovered at 350 degrees for 25 minutes. *Serves 6.*

MEAL-IN-ONE CHICKEN SALAD

4 whole chicken breasts, cooked and chilled
1 14-ounce can chicken broth
⅓ cup heavy cream
¾ cup mayonnaise
1 tablespoon chopped chives
½ teaspoon salt
Dash pepper
1 cup chopped celery
1 1-pound can French-style stringbeans, drained
4 medium tomatoes, sliced
½ cup Italian salad dressing
Chilled lettuce cups
4 hard-cooked eggs, sliced
12 ripe olives, sliced
Sprigs of parsley

Simmer chicken breasts in broth until tender. Remove chicken and chill. Cut several long strips from chicken breasts for garnish. Cube remainder of the meat and set aside. Whip heavy cream and stir in mayonnaise; season with chives, salt, and pepper, then fold in celery and chicken cubes. Chill. Marinate stringbeans and tomatoes separately in ¼ cup salad dressing each for 1 hour. Place lettuce cups on 4 plates and place a circle of tomatoes on each, then spoon on mounds of stringbeans. Divide chicken mixture and pile onto stringbeans, pressing into rounded shape with a spoon. Decorate with reserved chicken strips, egg slices, olives, and parsley. *Serves 4.*

SALADS

CURRY-COOL CHICKEN SALAD

3 whole chicken breasts
1½ cups diced unpared
   green apple
½ cup chopped green pepper
½ cup chopped celery
1 tablespoon chopped
   green onion
¾ cup mayonnaise
3 tablespoons light cream
½ teaspoon curry powder
Dash white pepper
Crisp lettuce leaves
1 teaspoon salt
⅛ teaspoon pepper

Simmer chicken breasts in water seasoned with salt and pepper until tender. Remove skin and bones and cut meat into cubes. Combine with apple, green pepper, celery, and green onion. In another bowl combine mayonnaise, cream, curry powder, and white pepper, mixing well. Blend dressing with chicken mixture and refrigerate until well chilled. Serve on beds of crisp lettuce. Serves 6.

FESTIVE CHRISTMAS STAR

1¼ cups cold chicken broth
1 tablespoon unflavored
   gelatin
3 tablespoons lemon juice
1 teaspoon salt
1 teaspoon sugar
½ cup mayonnaise
½ cup finely diced celery
¼ cup finely diced pimiento
¼ cup chopped green ends
   of green onion
1½ cups diced cooked
   chicken or turkey
Watercress
Cranberry slices
Pimiento-stuffed green olives

Bring 1 cup chicken broth to boil. Soften gelatin in ¼ cup cold broth, then dissolve in boiling broth. Add lemon juice, salt, sugar, and mayonnaise. Blend well, and refrigerate until mixture begins to set. Fold in celery, pimiento, green onion, and chicken, then turn into a 1½-quart star-shaped mold that has been rinsed with cold water. Chill until set. Before serving, unmold onto a bed of chilled watercress; decorate with cranberry slices and olives. Serves 6.

SUMMER SALAD MOLD

1 3- to 3½-pound fryer, with giblets
1 medium onion, halved
1 stalk celery, halved
1 small bay leaf
1 teaspoon Bouquet Garni
1 tablespoon salt
4 peppercorns
1 envelope unflavored gelatin
½ cup Chablis
1 teaspoon seasoned salt
2 hard-cooked eggs, sliced
6 pimiento-stuffed green olives, sliced
1 tablespoon mayonnaise

Place chicken and giblets in a saucepan; add onion, celery, bay leaf, Bouquet Garni, salt, peppercorns, and water to cover. Bring to a boil, reduce heat, cover, and simmer until chicken is tender. Remove chicken, cool broth, and skim off fat. When chicken is cool enough to handle, remove skin and bones, slice the breast meat, and chop the remaining meat. Soften gelatin in ¼ cup reserved chicken broth, then dissolve over hot water. Combine Chablis with 1 cup reserved chicken broth, add seasoned salt, and stir in gelatin. Pour ⅓ of gelatin mix into a 1-quart loaf pan and chill until set. Place only center slices of eggs and olives in a design over gelatin, reserving end pieces, then spread sliced white meat on top. Cover with ⅓ of gelatin and chill until set. Chill remaining gelatin slightly and add chopped chicken; chop end pieces of eggs and olives and add along with mayonnaise for last layer. Chill until firm, then unmold and slice. *Serves 4 to 6.*

16
SANDWICHES

MONTE CRISTO SANDWICH

12 slices white bread, with crusts removed
10 tablespoons butter, softened
8 slices American cheese
8 slices cooked chicken

4 slices baked ham
2 eggs
¼ cup light cream
¼ teaspoon salt
Parsley sprigs

Spread bread slices with butter on one side, reserving 2 tablespoons of the butter. Place 1 slice cheese on each of 4 bread slices and top each with 2 slices of chicken. Set 4 slices of bread, buttered side down, on the chicken and spread top side with remaining butter. Place a ham slice and a slice of cheese on this layer, and top with remaining bread, buttered side down. Cut sandwiches in half diagonally. Beat together eggs, cream, and salt. Melt remaining butter over low heat on a griddle. Dip sandwich triangles in egg to cover and grill until lightly browned. Place triangles on an ungreased baking sheet in a 400-degree oven and bake for 5 minutes. Garnish with parsley sprigs. *Serves 4.*

SANDWICHES

CHICKEN LUNCHEON QUICKS

4 slices bacon
2 English muffins, split
1 tablespoon butter
4 thin slices tomato
1 5-ounce jar boned chicken

1 can condensed cream of
  chicken soup, undiluted
½ cup shredded Cheddar
  cheese

Fry bacon on one side only, drain, and cut in half. Spread split muffins with butter and place under broiler on a shallow baking dish until golden. Place 1 slice of tomato on each muffin, and divide chicken among them. Stir soup until smooth and pour equal amounts on each muffin. Sprinkle with Cheddar cheese, then place 2 half-pieces of bacon side by side, uncooked side up, on top. Broil slowly until bacon is cooked. *Serves 4.*

CHICKEN TOSTADAS

4 tortillas
Salad oil for frying
2 cups cooked chicken,
  cut in strips
2 tablespoons butter
2 teaspoons soy sauce
2 cups shredded chilled
  lettuce

1 cantaloupe
1 avocado
1 tomato
1 canned green chili pepper
2 tablespoons chopped onion
1 teaspoon salt
2 tablespoons wine vinegar

Fry tortillas in a little salad oil until crisp. Drain well on paper towels. Heat chicken over low heat in butter and soy sauce. Place a tortilla on each of 4 salad plates, spread chicken over each and top with shredded lettuce. Cut 4 ½-inch-thick rings from cantaloupe; remove rinds by cutting in a zigzag design and place 1 ring on each salad. Cut melon balls from remaining cantaloupe and set aside for garnish. Peel and pit avocado; place in blender. Peel and quarter tomato and add along with chili pepper, onion, salt, and vinegar, then blend until smooth. Spread some of this mixture on each melon slice, and top with melon balls. *Serves 4.*

CREAMED CHICKEN AND HAM SANDWICHES

4 tablespoons butter
¼ cup flour
1 teaspoon seasoned salt
Dash pepper
2 cups milk
3 tablespoons dry sherry
¼ cup grated Cheddar cheese
2 cups cooked chicken, diced
Dash paprika
4 English muffins
8 slices cooked ham

Melt butter in saucepan. Stir in flour, seasoned salt, and pepper, then gradually stir in milk and continue stirring until thickened. Add sherry and Cheddar cheese, then gently fold in chicken and paprika. Simmer over low heat until ready to serve. Meanwhile, split, butter, and toast English muffins. Heat ham slices quickly in a pan and place on muffin halves. Top with prepared creamed chicken and serve immediately. *Serves 4.*

ELEGANT COMBINATION SANDWICH

2 3-ounce packages cream cheese, softened
¼ cup crumbled blue cheese
½ cup minced canned mushrooms
6 slices white bread
⅔ cup mayonnaise
⅓ cup minced green olives
1 teaspoon grated onion
6 slices whole wheat bread
12 large slices cooked chicken
Crisp lettuce leaves
6 large, thin slices tomato
12 stuffed green olives

Blend cream cheese with blue cheese and mushrooms until smooth. Spread on white bread slices. Blend mayonnaise with minced olives and onion and spread on whole wheat slices. Place 2 slices of chicken on top of each whole wheat slice, cover with lettuce, top with a tomato slice, and reverse spread pieces of white bread to make a sandwich. Carefully cut each sandwich in half diagonally and hold together with toothpicks topped with stuffed olives. *Serves 6.*

SANDWICHES

FRENCH-TOASTED CHICKEN SANDWICHES

1 10½-ounce can prepared seasoned white sauce
1 cup minced cooked chicken
Tiny pinch tarragon
8 slices white bread
2 eggs
1 cup milk
¼ teaspoon salt
Dash pepper
Butter for frying

Heat white sauce in the top of a double boiler, stirring until smooth. Add chicken and tarragon and heat through. Spread mixture on 4 slices of bread, and top with remaining bread. In a shallow dish beat together eggs, milk, salt, and pepper. Dip each sandwich in the mixture to cover thoroughly, then place on buttered griddle and fry until golden, turning only once. *Serves 4.*

FROSTED SANDWICH LOAF

1 loaf unsliced sandwich bread
4 ounces (1 stick) butter, softened
2 cans deviled ham
2 tablespoons mayonnaise, plus ⅓ cup
1 13½-ounce can pineapple tidbits
1 cup minced cooked chicken
¼ cup sweet pickle relish
1 cup crunch-style peanut butter
1 8-ounce package cream cheese, softened
1 5-ounce jar Kraft "Old English" sharp cheese spread
1 2-ounce jar pimiento-stuffed green olives, sliced

Trim crust from bread and cut into three lengthwise slices. Butter 1 side of each slice using all the butter, and place 1 slice on a platter, buttered side up. Combine deviled ham with 2 tablespoons mayonnaise and spread on top. Drain pineapple well, reserving 1 tablespoon liquid; crush ½ cup of the tidbits and drain again, then spread on ham mixture. Place the second slice of bread, buttered side up, on the pineapple. Combine chicken, ⅓ cup mayonnaise, and pickle relish, and spread on second layer. Spread peanut butter on buttered side of third slice and place upside down on top of chicken spread. Combine cream cheese, cheese spread, and 1 tablespoon pineapple liquid and beat until fluffy. Cover top and sides of loaf with this frosting. Place remaining pineapple tidbits on absorbent paper, then decorate top of loaf with alternating diagonal stripes of pineapple and olives. Chill for at least 1 hour before slicing. *Serves 8.*

KNIFE AND FORK SANDWICH

3 tablespoons butter
6 slices rye bread
1½ cups shredded lettuce
6 slices Swiss cheese
1 cup thinly sliced cucumber
6 large or 12 small slices cooked chicken
6 tablespoons Thousand Island dressing
3 hard-cooked eggs, sliced

Butter 1 side of each slice of bread. Top each with lettuce, a slice of Swiss cheese, some cucumber slices, chicken, 1 tablespoon of the dressing. Decorate with slices of hard-cooked egg. *Serves 6.*

TOPLESS CURRIED CHICKEN SANDWICHES

4 slices buttered toast
8 slices cooked chicken
Salt
Pepper
2 tablespoons cranberry sauce
½ cup mayonnaise
¼ cup minced celery
¼ cup minced green onion
½ cup shredded, pared tart apple
½ teaspoon curry powder

Place toast on baking sheet, buttered side up. Arrange chicken on toast, and sprinkle with salt and pepper. Spread with a thin layer of cranberry sauce. Combine remaining ingredients with ¼ teaspoon salt and spread over chicken. Place sheet 8 inches from broiler flame and heat 6 to 8 minutes, or until delicately browned. *Serves 4.*

SANDWICHES

DREAMY CHICKEN LIVER SANDWICHES

1 pound fresh chicken livers
4 tablespoons butter
2 tablespoons finely chopped onion
½ green pepper, chopped
1 avocado
1 cup sour cream
1 teaspoon Worcestershire sauce
1 teaspoon salt
¼ teaspoon pepper
4 English muffins

Wash and drain chicken livers. Melt butter in skillet, then, over low heat, sauté chicken livers, onion, and green pepper for 15 minutes, or until livers reach desired doneness. Cut 4 slices from avocado and dice remainder. Gently stir in diced avocado, sour cream, Worcestershire sauce, salt, and pepper. Heat, but do not boil. Split and toast English muffins, spoon chicken liver mixture on top, and decorate with avocado slices. *Serves 4.*

SUNDAY SUPPER SANDWICHES

½ cup chopped green onion
2 tablespoons butter
1 can cream of mushroom soup, undiluted
½ cup milk
2 cups diced cooked chicken
6 slices white bread, toasted
6 slices American cheese
6 thick slices tomato
1 cup grated Parmesan cheese

Sauté onion in butter for 5 minutes. Stir in soup and milk, add chicken, and heat through. Arrange toast in a single layer in a shallow baking dish, place a slice of American cheese on each slice of toast, then spread creamed chicken on top. Place a tomato slice on each serving and sprinkle with Parmesan cheese. Broil until lightly golden and bubbling. *Serves 3 or 6.*

INDEX

A La King, 93
Appetizers, 11–14; Chicken Livers, 11; Chicken Livers *en Brochette*, 12; Crisp Oriental, 13; Pâté de Foie, 14; Picnic Pâté, 13; Timbales with Tomato Sauce, 12–13
Applejack Chicken, 122
Arroz Con Pollo, 98–99
Artichokes, Chicken with Rosé, 125
Asparagus, Creamed Chicken with, 91
Austrian Chicken, 100
Avocado, Chicken Newburg, 90–91

Baked Chicken, 23–29; African, 98; Curry-Glazed, 24–25; Deviled Wings, 25; Easy Tarragon, 25; Garlic, 26; Maryland, 23–24; Old-Fashioned Oven-Fried, 26; Oven-Barbecued, 27; Pakistani, 115; Rosy, 85; San Francisco, 28; Simply Delicious, 27; "Souper," 29; Stuffed Legs, 28; Tasty Tarragon Wings, 26
Barbecued, New England, 33; Oven, 27; with Sesame Soy, 34

Boning, 5–6
Braised Chicken Breasts, 80
Brandied Chicken Shell, 123
Bread Sauce, 104
Brioches, Swiss Chicken-Filled, 110–111
Broccoli, Chicken Casserole, 81–82
Broiled Chicken, 31–37; French Quarter, 31; Glazed Rotisserie, 32; Luau Drumsticks, 34; New England Barbecued, 33; Rotisserie Intrigue, 33; Sonoma, 32
Broth, 17
Buying, 2

Cacciatora, 72; Busy-Day, 70
Capers, Italian Chicken with, 107–108
Capon, Complete Dinner, 39–40; with Cheese Sauce, 41; Shanghai, 41
Carving, 7
Casseroles, 57–68; Alsace, 57; American-Style Risotto, 58–59; Chicken Liver, 76–77; Chicken Under a Blanket, 64; Clambake, 58; Dixie

151

INDEX

Casseroles (*cont'd.*)
  with Cornpone, 67; Double-Crust Pie, 61–62; Fiesta, 68; French with Dumplings, 59; Hostess's Favorite, 64–65; Individual Soufflés, 60; Make-Ahead, 67; Minute Pie, 63; Mornay *en Casserole,* 61; Potluck Supper, 65; Quick Rarebit, 66; Spring Chicken Soufflé, 66; Tamale Pie, 60; Tetrazzini, 63; Vegetable, 62
Central American Chicken with Swiss Chard, 101
Chafing Dish Chicken, 90
Cheese Sauce, Chicken-Rice Casserole, 87
Chicken Breasts, 79–87; Braised, 80; Broccoli Casserole, 81–82; Chicken-Rice Casserole with Cheese Sauce, 87; Curried with Vegetables, 79; Fisherman's Wharf, 85; Fruit Medley, 80; Gala, 81; with Ham, 86; Jubilee, 82; Kiev, 82–83; Pecan-Stuffed, 36–37; Pago Pago, 83; Perigourdine, 86–87; Rosy Baked, 85; Skillet Party Chicken, 84; Sophisticated Chicken Sauté, 83; *Sous Cloche,* 107
Chicken Livers, Creamed on Toast, 89; *En Brochette,* 12; Filling for Omelet, 74; Party Casserole, 76–77; Risotto, 75; Sandwich, 150; Sautéed in Wine Sauce, 124
Chicken-Noodle Casserole, 74; Alla Romana, 97
Chicken-Rice Casserole with Cheese Sauce, 87
Chicken Roll with Mornay Sauce, 95
Chinese Walnut Chicken, 102
Chow Mein, 103
Cider, Costa Rican Chicken in, 123–124
Cleaning, 4–5
Coconut Chicken in Spinach, 102–103
Compote of Chicken Marsala, 125
Costa Rican Chicken in Cider, 123–124

Couscous, North African, 114–115
Crab, Stuffed Chicken Halves, 42; Chicken Boats, 91–92
Creamed Chicken, 89–95; À La King, 93; with Asparagus, 91; Avocado Newburg, 90–91; Chafing Dish, 90; Chicken Roll with Mornay Sauce, 95; Crab, 91–92; Elegant, 94; and Ham Sandwich, 147; Livers, 89; Pancakes, 93–94; Swiss Crêpes, 92–93
Creole, Chicken Gumbo, 17; Caribbean, 73
Crêpes, Swiss Chicken, 92–93
Croquettes, 29–30
Curried Chicken, and Vegetable Skillet, 79; Glazed, 24–25; Last Minute, 71
Cutting, 5

Deviled Chicken Wings, 25
Dressing, Green Goddess, 139
Drumsticks, Luau, 34
Duck, Casserole with Spanish Chicken and Seafood, 109

Enchiladas with Chili Sauce, 106
English Roast Chicken with Bread Sauce, 104
Equador Orange Chicken, 119

Freshness of Chicken, 3
Fricassee, Chicken Stew, 49
Fried Chicken, 29–30; Crisp-Fried, 30; Croquettes, 29–30; Deep-Fried, 30
Fruit Medley and Chicken Breasts, 80
Frying, 8

Game Hens, 129–135; Butter-Barbecued, 134; Cold Brandied with Peaches, 132; Far Eastern Steamed, 130; Flaming Roast with Cherries, 130–131; German with Sauerkraut, 131–132; Island, 129; Picnic, 132–133; Potted with Vege-

INDEX

tables, 133; Raphael Weill, 134–135; with Wild Rice Stuffing, 131
Garlic Baked Chicken, 26
General rules for cooking, 8–10
Greek Roast Chicken, 106
Green Goddess Dressing, 139
Grilled Chicken, Barbecue Sesame Soy, 34; Calypso Platter with Spanish Rice, 34–35; Chef's Special, 35; Giddy with Gooseberry Sauce, 36; Pecan-Stuffed Breasts, 36–37; Polynesian on Spit, 37
Grilling, 9
Gold Coast Chicken Stew, 104–105
Gumbo, 55; Creole Gumbo, 17

Ham and Chicken, 86
Haitian Chicken Soup, 100
Hash with Mushroom Sauce, 69
Hens (see Game Hens)
Hollander's Pie 108–109
Hors d'oeuvres, Chicken Liver, 11
Hungarian Paprikash, 110

Indian Korma, 114
International, 97–120
Italian Chicken with Capers, 107–108

Japanese Chicken Bundles, 105

Kiev, 82–83

Makaha Mountain, 112
Malayan Chicken with Pork, 111
Marchand de Vin, 122
Marsala, Compote of, 125
Maryland Baked Chicken, 23–24

Nasi Goreng, 112–113
Noodles and Chicken Alla Romana, 97
North African, Couscous, 114–115; Roast, 118–119

Old-Fashioned Stew with Dumplings, 53–54

Omelet with Chicken Liver Filling, 74
Orange Chicken from Equador, 119
Orange Sauce, Spicy, 71

Pakistani Baked Chicken, 115
Pancakes, Chicken Filled, 93–94
Pâté de Foie, 14; Picnic Pâté, 13; Pâté Salad Mold, 138
Persian Joojeh, 115–116
Phillippine Adobo, 116
Pie, Chicken, Double-Crust, 61–62; Hollander's, 108–109; Minute, 63
Pilaf, 77
Polynesian Chicken on Spit, 37
Pork, Malayan Chicken with, 111
Preparation for cooking, 4

Quantity of Chicken, 4

Rarebit, Quick, 66
Red Wine, Spicy Chicken in, 127
Roast Chicken, 39–47; with Bread Stuffing, 104; Greek, 106; with Meat-Rice Stuffing, 42–43; North African, 118–119; with Nut Stuffing, 40
Roasting, 8–9
Rotisserie, Glazed, 32; Intrigue, 33

Salads, 137–143; Chicken-Almond, 139; Chicken Breasts in Aspic, 137–138; Curry-Cool, 142; Festive Christmas Star, 142; Frosted, 140; with Green Goddess Dressing, 139; Hot, 141; Meal-in-One, 141; Pacifica, 138; Pâté Mold, 138; Summer Mold, 143; and Vegetable, 140
Sandwiches, 145–150; Chicken Liver, 150; Creamed Chicken and Ham, 147; Elegant Combination, 147; French-Toasted, 148; Frosted Loaf, 148–149; Knife and Fork, 149; Luncheon Quicks, 146; Monte Cristo, 145; Sunday Supper, 150; Topless Curried, 149; Tostadas, 146
San Francisco Baked Chicken, 28

INDEX

Sauce, Orange, 71; Bread, 104
Sautéed Chicken, Livers in Wine Sauce, 124; Mellow, 124; Sophisticated, 83
Scotch Stovies, 116–117
Seafood, Spanish Chicken and Duck Casserole, 109
Singapore Chicken, 113
Skillet Entrees, 69–78; Busy-Day Cacciatora, 70; Cacciatora, 72; Caribbean Creole, 73; Chicken Liver Risotto, 75; Chicken-Noodle, 74; Chestnut Stew, 72; Cutlets with Sauce, 70–71; Exotic Spice, 73; Hash with Mushroom Sauce, 69; Last-Minute Curry, 71; Melted, 75; Omelet with Chicken Liver Filling, 74–75; Outrigger Special, 78; Party Chicken Liver, 76–77; Pilaf, 77; Skillet Lemon, 77; Smothered, 78; Spicy Orange Sauce, 71; Sweet and Sour, 76
Smothered Chicken, 78
Soufflés, Individual Casserole, 60; Palm, 99; Spring Chicken, 66
Soups, 15–21; Belgian, 19; Broth, 17; Chilled with Cucumber, 18; Continental, 15; Cream of Chicken, 18; Creole Chicken Gumbo, 17; Haitian One-Course, 100; Matzo-Ball, 21; Hurry-up Mulligatawny, 18; Mushroom, 16; Oriental Chicken-Corn, 20; Scotch Chicken-Leek, 20; Winter Harvest, 19–20; Won Ton, 16
Sour Cream, Ukranian Chicken with, 118
South American Pollo Asado, 119–120
South Seas Stew, 105
Southern Chicken Stew, 52
Spanish Chicken, Duck and Seafood Casserole, 109; with Coconut 102–103
Spicy Chicken in Red Wine, 127

Stew, 49–55; in Beer, 50–51; with Chestnuts, 72; Fricassee, 49; Fricassee with Meatballs, 50; Gold Coast, 104–105; Gumbo, 55; Old-Fashioned with Dumplings, 53–54; Paisano with Polenta, 54; Peasant Dinner, 52; South Seas, 105; Southern, 52; Vegetable, 51
Stewing, 10
Story of Chicken, The, 1
Stovies, Scotch, 116–117
Stuffing, 6–7
Stuffings, Cabbage, 43; Corn, 43; Cornbread-Walnut, 47; Crab, 42; Island, 47; Indian, 44; Meat Mixture, 44; Mushroom-Herb, 46; Nut, 40; Oyster, 46–47; Raw Potato, 45; Sausage-Apple, 45; Scandinavian, 45; Wild Rice, 46
Supremes de Poulet, 117–118
Sweet and Sour Chicken, 76
Swiss Chard, Central American Chicken with, 101

Tacos, 101–102
Tarragon Baked Chicken, 25
Temperature, Roasting, 8
Tetrazzini, 63
Timbales, 12; with Tomato Sauce, 12–13
Time, Roasting, 8
Trussing, 7
Types of Chicken, 3

Ukranian Chicken in Sour Cream, 118

Vegetables, Curried Chicken with, 79
Véronique, 121
Vineyard Chicken, 126

Walnut Chicken, Chinese, 102
Winebibber's Chicken, 126
Winebibber's Corner, 121–127
Won Ton, 16